The DISSERTATION *Journey*

A Practical and Comprehensive Guide to Planning, Writing, and Defending Your Dissertation

CAROL M. ROBERTS

CORWIN
A SAGE Company

For information:

Corwin
A SAGE Company
2455 Teller Road
Thousand Oaks, California 91320
(800) 233-9936
Fax: (800) 417-2466
www.corwin.com

SAGE India Pvt. Ltd.
B 1/I 1 Mohan Cooperative
 Industrial Area
Mathura Road, New Delhi 110 044
India

SAGE Ltd.
1 Oliver's Yard
55 City Road
London EC1Y 1SP
United Kingdom

SAGE Asia-Pacific Pte. Ltd.
33 Pekin Street #02-01
Far East Square
Singapore 048763

Printed in the United States of America

Library of Congress Cataloging-in-Publication Data

Roberts, Carol M.
The dissertation journey : a practical and comprehensive guide to planning, writing, and defending your dissertation / Carol M. Roberts. — 2nd ed.
    p. cm.
Includes bibliographical references and index.
ISBN 978-1-4129-7798-2 (pbk.)
    1. Doctor of education degree—Handbooks, manuals, etc. 2. Dissertations, Academic—Handbooks, manuals, etc. 3. Report writing—Handbooks, manuals, etc. I. Title.

LB1742.R63 2010
808'.066378—dc22   2010020319

This book is printed on acid-free paper.

14 15 16 17   10 9 8 7 6

Acquisitions Editor:	Dan Alpert
Associate Editor:	Megan Bedell
Editorial Assistant:	Sarah Bartlett
Production Editor:	Amy Schroller
Copy Editor:	Jenifer Dill
Typesetter:	C&M Digitals (P) Ltd.
Proofreader:	Theresa Kay
Indexer:	Molly Hall
Cover Designer:	Michael Dubowe

Contents

Foreword

When I completed reading *The Dissertation Journey* by Carol Roberts, my first reaction was, "Where was this book 20 years ago when I started directing dissertations?" My second reaction was, "Heck, where was this book even before then when I wrote my own dissertation?" My third reaction was, "Every doctoral student in our department needs to read this book." And my fourth reaction was, "So does every faculty member."

Dr. Roberts's book provides insight into every aspect of developing and writing a dissertation. From selecting a topic, to choosing a committee, to deciding what research approach to use, to the actual writing and defense of the dissertation, Dr. Roberts provides clear and comprehensive directions for any student faced with the challenge of writing a dissertation. I particularly appreciate how she methodically takes students through each chapter that will comprise the dissertation, not only providing an overview of what each should contain but also offering helpful suggestions and checklists to reinforce what constitutes a good dissertation.

A really appealing component of *The Dissertation Journey* is the information provided to doctoral students on how to use technology to support development of a dissertation. Not only does Dr. Roberts offer good suggestions on how to use the computer in writing a dissertation, she provides a listing of electronic and Internet sources students can use to access research materials and articles.

Furthermore, the section that Dr. Roberts provides on the ethics of writing a dissertation is a must read for any doctoral student. She reminds the reader of copyright laws, clearly defines plagiarism and how to avoid it, and highlights the importance of understanding and observing the rules governing research on human subjects.

Finally, Dr. Roberts provides a great concluding section that focuses on students' responsibilities once the dissertation is done and they have graduated. She not only encourages them to share their research findings broadly but also challenges the students to use their experience to mentor others undertaking the rigors of a doctoral degree.

Returning to my initial comments, I found *The Dissertation Journey* to be a wonderfully useful tool to assist both doctoral students and graduate faculty through the dissertation development process. The work is very clearly written and addresses every aspect of dissertation writing. It is so good that I plan to have all of my doctoral students purchase and read the work. It will save them, as well as me, a lot of lost time, gnashing of teeth, and heartache.

Dr. Roberts is to be congratulated for adding this important work to the field. There is no doubt that, if doctoral students and their advisors will use this composition as a guide in developing dissertations, the quality of research in higher education across the country will be immensely enhanced.

Kenneth R. Stevenson

Professor, Department of
Educational Leadership and Policies

University of South Carolina

New to This Edition

I am very pleased to have the opportunity to write a second edition of my book, *The Dissertation Journey: A Practical and Comprehensive Guide to Planning, Writing, and Defending Your Dissertation*. This updated and expanded edition includes not only new information that is vital to navigating the dissertation process, it also includes an expansion of previous topics for greater clarity and utility.

New features added to this second edition include the following:

1. **A new chapter titled "What Are the Ethical Considerations in Research?"** In this chapter, I discuss the central ethical issues involved in conducting research relative to human rights, data collection, data analysis and interpretation, respect for the research site, writing, and disseminating the research.

2. **New information about the process, importance, and purpose of developing a theoretical or conceptual framework.** It includes responses to questions such as, "What is a conceptual or theoretical framework?" "How does a conceptual framework differ from a theoretical framework?" "Why do you need a conceptual or theoretical framework?" and "How do you find a conceptual or theoretical framework?" Also provided are examples from dissertations for greater understanding.

3. **A completely revised and updated chapter titled "Using the Internet and Technology to Conduct Research."** Since more and more researchers use the Internet and technology for all phases of dissertation writing, I incorporated in this second edition new web-based technologies. New information about search engines, evaluating websites, and social networking on the web is also included.

4. **A completely revised and expanded chapter on reviewing the literature.** I expanded the steps in conducting a literature review

from four to eight and added considerably more detail to the process. An updated list of secondary sources and style manuals widely used in the social sciences is incorporated.

5. **A thorough update of all websites and references, including new editions of works.**

Preface

Today, colleges and universities offer master's and doctoral degrees in increasing numbers. Many students enroll in these programs, and in many cases, they do not receive appropriate guidance and support in conceptualizing, conducting, and writing an original research study. This is evidenced by an estimated 40% to 50% of doctoral students nationwide who complete their course work but not the final act of writing their dissertation. They become ABDs (all-but-dissertation). This represents a tremendous waste of time, money, and energy.

In reviewing the literature, I discovered very few useful, comprehensive books that guide master's or doctoral students through the formidable and demanding process of crafting a high-quality research study. This book offers the practical guidance often lacking in doctoral programs and in the literature about planning, writing, and defending a dissertation. Doctoral students need to (1) get a clear picture of what it takes to write a high-quality research study and see it as doable; (2) understand it as a psychological and human relations venture as much as a research exercise; (3) feel encouraged and supported in their efforts; (4) experience the process as a satisfying, rewarding, and exciting journey; and (5) finish!

I wrote this book to satisfy the existing need for a clear, concise, cut-to-the-chase guidebook for completing a doctoral dissertation. *The Dissertation Journey* provides a step-by-step guide on how to plan, write, and defend a dissertation. Its structure parallels the dissertation process and presents detailed information about the content and process from conceptualizing a topic to publishing the results. It addresses the psychological and emotional barriers students confront and provides up-to-date information on using the computer and the Internet in the various stages of dissertating. The style is personal, informal, and conversational—much like a coach talking one-on-one with a student. To enhance learning and clarify concepts, I included a myriad of examples together with helpful hints, checklists, and quotations. Since writing a dissertation can be a bewildering and overwhelming experience for students, I use the metaphor of climbing a mountain for inspiration and to maintain interest and motivation to persevere in spite of obstacles.

For the past 22 years, I have had the opportunity to teach doctoral students at the University of La Verne—a premier doctoral program in California known for its innovative approach to educating leaders. The faculty provides a relevant, practical, and high-quality program focused on helping students succeed in completing their dissertation. The one-to-one coaching, group tutorials, videos, online discussions, webinars, and research seminars are exemplary techniques for teaching the dissertation process. As a result, our students' graduation rate is 81%—almost twice that of the national average.

The Dissertation Journey: A Practical and Comprehensive Guide to Planning, Writing, and Defending Your Dissertation incorporates many approaches and techniques taught in the University of La Verne's doctoral program. These techniques, plus the insights and knowledge I gained from years of experience teaching and guiding dissertation students, serve as a valuable road map for the dissertation journey and, hopefully, make the task more understandable, easier, more enjoyable, and less time-consuming. This is not a complete work on writing dissertations, nor could it be; the scope would be overwhelming. The book does not include detailed information on certain aspects of academic research, such as design and methodology, data analysis techniques, or writing style and mechanics. I reference appropriate books that concentrate on these technical areas.

This book is geared toward the specific needs and concerns of doctoral students as they proceed through each step of the dissertation process. It focuses primarily on the social sciences; however, graduate students in most academic disciplines desiring to complete a research study should find the book's content useful and applicable. Generally, the steps for writing a thesis and a dissertation are much the same regardless of the topic or discipline; they vary primarily in scope and complexity. Graduate faculty involved with student research should also find the book's ideas and suggestions beneficial. It eliminates the need to answer over and over again those questions that students routinely ask. Universities vary considerably in their dissertation requirements and procedures. In addition, there is considerable diversity among the preferences of advisors and departments within a university. The suggestions offered in this book should not be considered final, nor should they preempt the judgment and opinions of research advisors and committees.

Researching and writing a thesis or dissertation should be an enjoyable and rewarding experience—one students can comprehend and most of all complete. There is a better way than letting half or more of our nation's doctoral students become ABDs. It is my hope that this book, with its straight talk, step-by-step guidance, and practical advice, will make the journey to "doctor" smoother and, in the process, help beat the overwhelming odds of ABDism.

A Note to Doctoral Candidates

Greetings! You are embarking on a new and exciting journey—obtaining a doctoral degree. This journey requires completing a dissertation, the pinnacle of academic achievement. In many ways, the journey is like climbing a high mountain; it is a long and arduous trek—not for the fainthearted. It is fraught with hazards and obstacles along the path that can dampen your spirit. However, it also offers incomparable opportunities for personal and professional growth.

Reaching the summit of a mountain symbolizes the process you go through to complete your dissertation. The climb tests your mettle and challenges your resolve, but once you complete it and experience the magnificent view from the top, you realize the rewards far outweigh the effort. The exhilaration and pride of accomplishment, the fulfillment that results from contribution, a deeper self-awareness, and greater confidence in yourself as a scholar are just a few of the rewards that await you.

I remember well the experience of seeing my own dissertation as a looming mountain before me—massive and awesome—with the accompanying feelings of doubt and apprehension. I learned, as you will, that journeying to the peak is more than an intellectual pilgrimage, it is also an emotional and psychological one. It requires commitment, perseverance, stamina, and mental toughness—more than you ever thought you had.

Completing a dissertation changes your life. I discovered that my primary reward was not so much the exhilaration of standing on top of the mountain at journey's end, but rather who I became as a result of the climb. Only by taking yourself to the limit can you know what you're made of. "It is not the mountain we conquer, but ourselves" (Sir Edmund Hillary, one of the first men to reach the summit of Mount Everest).

I wrote this book to help make your journey to the summit a satisfying and rewarding one. In these pages, I speak to you informally as an advisor and friend about the entire dissertation process. Plus, I speak about those critical issues related to the personal and social side of dissertating (organization, time management, human relations, etc.).

The material presented in this book represents years spent guiding dissertation students, dialoguing with faculty colleagues, and researching the literature on this topic. Please remember that the ideas and recommendations provided should be used only as a guide. Your advisor and committee are the ultimate sources of information and opinion about your dissertation.

It is my hope that you catch summit fever and become utterly motivated to reach the top. Do bring a spirit of adventure to this journey, and by all means, enjoy the climb! Warmest regards and good luck!

Acknowledgments

No one climbs a high mountain alone. Experience and expertise, support and encouragement are all needed. I am indebted to many people who provided these necessities, which helped make this book a reality. I am most appreciative of the assistance and contributions of my professional colleagues in the University of La Verne's Doctoral Program in Organizational Leadership, with whom I have worked for the past 22 years. They freely share their wisdom and knowledge, from which I learn so much.

I would like to acknowledge and thank Drs. William Bearley, Donald Clague, James Cox, Thomas Harvey, William Paulo, and Barbara Peterson. Through their insightful presentations at doctoral seminars, faculty exchanges, and personal coaching, they provided foundational information on preparing the core chapters of the dissertation (Chapters 1 through 5). Many of the ideas expressed in these five sections of the book encapsulate the collective wisdom of these talented individuals, who, over the years, contributed greatly to the quality of our doctoral program and to my own intellectual growth and development.

I also give special thanks to Mary Townsend, Donna Bentley, Clive Houston Brown, Donald Hays, and Larry Kemper, who provided feedback and constructive suggestions for improving this work. For the second edition, I wish to thank Donna Bentley, Librarian at the University of La Verne, for her valuable help in revising and updating the Internet and technology resources. I also appreciate the support and encouragement to pursue this project given by Drs. Barbara Poling, Department Chair, and Leonard Pellicer, Dean of the College of Education and Organizational Leadership at the University of La Verne.

I also want to thank those doctoral students whom I have had the privilege of instructing—and particularly those who invited me to chair their dissertations and serve on their committees. They helped me understand the unique challenges associated with conducting high-quality research and provided many helpful comments and suggestions that are incorporated in this book.

My greatest debt is to my husband, Edward, who gives me the love and confidence to leave "base camp" for the many physical and inward climbs I choose to make.

The contributions of the following reviewers are gratefully acknowledged.

Martha A. Alcock
Professor of Education
Capital University
Columbus, OH

Betty J. Alford
Associate Professor
Stephen F. Austin State University
Nacogdoches, TX

Jim Allen
Professor of Educational
    Psychology
Thelma P. Lally School of Education
The College of Saint Rose
Albany, NY

Robert B. Amenta
Director of Education
    Administration
California Lutheran University
Thousand Oaks, CA

Sharon Toomey Clark
Educational Consultant
Clark & Associates
Claremont, CA

Michelle Collay
School Coach
Bay Area Coalition for Equitable
    Schools
Oakland, CA

Larry E. Decker
C. S. Mott Professor of
    Community Education
Florida Atlantic University
Boca Raton, FL

Roxana DellaVecchia
Assistant Dean
College of Education, Towson
Towson, MD

Sarah Edwards
Assistant Professor
Teacher Education Department
University of Nebraska at
    Omaha
Omaha, NE

Douglas Fisher
Associate Professor
San Diego State University
San Diego, CA

Margaret A. (Peggie) Price
Assistant Professor in
    Curriculum and Instruction
Texas Tech University
Lubbock, TX

About the Author

 **Carol M. Roberts** is a professor in the University of La Verne's Doctoral Program in Organizational Leadership, where she advises doctoral students, chairs dissertations, and teaches research plus a variety of courses focused on leading organizations. Carol is a speaker, consultant, and seminar leader specializing in organizational and team development, strategic planning, conflict resolution, coaching, and personal mastery. She has been a trainer for the California School Leadership Academy and the California School Boards Association. She received her doctoral degree in planning, policy, and administration from the University of Southern California. Carol served on the Executive Board for the Southern Counties Women in Educational Management and was awarded its Woman of the Year award.

PART I

Quests and Questions

Lives of great men all remind us

We can make our lives sublime,

And, departing, leave behind us

Footprints on the sands of time.

—Henry Wadsworth Longfellow

1

Do You Have
What It Takes?

Why Take This Journey?

Throughout the ages, people have pursued the upper limits of their capabilities. They have answered the call to adventure, learning, and high achievement. Completing the dissertation journey is an adventure in learning and personal growth, the outcome of which can result in extraordinary accomplishment and contribution. Unquestionably, obtaining an EdD or a PhD is the summit of academia—the highest degree any university can bestow. This journey to "doctor" is difficult, with obstacles and demands along the way; however, once completed, the pride and exultation are a life-long affirmation.

> The heights by great men reached and kept were not obtained by sudden flight, but they, while their companions slept, were toiling upward in the night.
>
> —Longfellow

A doctorate usually requires completion of a dissertation that demonstrates your ability to plan, conduct, write, and defend an original research study. In many ways, the dissertation process is a journey not unlike climbing a difficult mountain. The journey is arduous and long, usually three to five years from beginning to end, and it is easy to become frustrated, exhausted, and discouraged. It is grueling—definitely not for anyone who lacks commitment or perseverance. Those who successfully scale the peak are those willing to put in long hours and hard work.

Writing a dissertation is a personal transformative experience and can be a peak experience—one of those life-fulfilling moments. Abraham Maslow (1968) referred to them as "moments of highest happiness and fulfillment" (p. 73) and added, "A peak experience is felt as a self-validating, self-justifying moment which carries its own intrinsic value with it" (p. 79). He claimed that the worth of the experience makes the pain worthwhile. Robert Schuller (1980) also talked about peak experiences in his book *The Peak to Peek Principle*. He called a peak experience "an experience of success, achievement, and accomplishment which feeds your self-esteem, which then expands your self-confidence" (p. 99) and added, "It's an experience that leaves you with an awareness that you are more than you ever thought you were" (p. 113).

These positive, uplifting, and inspiring words speak to the high accomplishment of completing a doctoral dissertation. Many high points and joys happen along the dissertation journey—some simple, some exhilarating. Moments such as realizing you really do have a researchable topic, having your proposal accepted, obtaining an acceptable questionnaire return rate, and creative moments and intellectual insights are all triumphs along the path. The instant your advisor calls you "doctor," the ecstasy of walking to "Pomp and Circumstance" at graduation, and when your doctoral hood is placed over your head are self-fulfilling, unforgettable moments that make the hard work and sacrifice worthwhile.

> Research has revealed that the attitude you have at the beginning of a task determines the outcome of that task more than any other single factor. For example, if you believe you will be able to succeed at a particular undertaking and you approach the endeavor with a sense of excitement and joyful expectation, your chances of achieving success are much higher than if you face the task with dread and apprehension.
>
> —Abascal, Brucato, and Brucato (2001, p. 39)

Unfortunately, there is a mythology that supports a negative view that completing a dissertation is drudgery and demeaning, consisting only of a series of hoops to jump through and hurdles to overcome. Students who adopt this mindset spend much of their time whining and "awfulizing" their experiences. They bemoan their plight and feel tormented throughout the entire process. It is a truism that completing a dissertation is hard work, time-consuming, frustrating, and, at times, frightening—this is a given. It takes a good deal of self-discipline and courage to undertake a project of this magnitude.

What makes the difference between a peak experience and a "heartbreak hill" experience? Attitude. Attitude is everything! On the mountain and in life, our attitude makes or breaks us. If you think you can do it, then you can.

Approaching the dissertation journey with a spirit of adventure, optimism, and a can-do attitude helps ensure that you will succeed and achieve a peak experience in the process. Climbing a mountain peak is a powerful metaphor; it represents the path to growth and transformation. The obstacles encountered along the way embody the challenges that help expand your thinking and your boundaries. The risks are substantial, the sacrifices great. However, the view is magnificent from the top, and it is reserved for those courageous adventurers who dare to challenge their own limits. Ultimately, though, it's the journey itself that results in "self-validative delight," not just standing at the top. Once you are there, you will not be the same person or ever again look at the world in the same light.

> The primary reward is not the goal but what you become as a result of doing all that was necessary to reach the goal.
>
> —David McNalley

With hard work and perseverance, "I'll see you at the top."

Do You Have What It Takes to Journey to the Peak?

Remember the travelers on the yellow brick road? They wanted to get to the Emerald City, yet each had to be transformed in order to get there. They needed three things to find their way: brains, heart, and courage. You will need the merging of these same three things to successfully complete your dissertation journey. Cognitive ability is necessary but not sufficient. Certainly, you must put all your intellectual powers to work in conducting your study and analyzing its results. Such powers do make for easier climbing. However, it's your heart—the spirit and passion you bring—that sustains you for the long haul. The third critical need is courage—the ability to dig deep into yourself and persevere when the going gets tough and you want to quit. You will find that when you think you cannot go another step, there is an untapped and astonishing reservoir of sustenance that can pull you through—mind over matter.

Answering the following questions honestly can help you better understand what it takes to climb the dissertation mountain—that final challenge to obtaining your doctorate. Just remember that you can, and probably will, accomplish more under sometimes adverse conditions than you may believe.

1. What Are You Willing to Sacrifice?

There is no true success in any large-scale endeavor without sacrifice. Self-denial is the name of the game. Are you willing to give up momentary pleasures for your long-term goal? To burn some midnight oil? Completing the dissertation is a demanding task and takes time, money, and energy, which can affect all aspects of your life. It can cause strained relationships with your spouse, partner, children, friends, and work colleagues. It can affect your work assignment, causing conflicts between time spent doing your dissertation and time spent doing your job. Be realistic about the financial costs connected with conducting a research study, such as typing, copying, library expenses, consultants, travel, postage, telephone calls, computer costs, and so on.

2. How Much Are You Willing to Endure?

The path is fraught with difficulties and obstacles. Can you face them without becoming discouraged? Are you prepared for the stress that accompanies emotional setbacks and extra demands on your time? The dissertation process is often obscure and perplexing, requiring a high level of tolerance for ambiguity and uncertainty. It means often working outside your comfort zone. Are you willing to risk the unknown and to be teachable? If not, you can wander around aimlessly in the foothills of confusion and frustration. Are you willing to learn as you go?

> That which we obtain too easily, we esteem too lightly.
>
> —Thomas Paine

It is important to recognize the downsides, the consequences, and the risks of taking the dissertation journey. If you believe that you have what it takes, you can climb the mountain, stand on the top, and feel the joy of high achievement.

Avoiding the Hazards of High-Altitude Climbing

Climbing real or metaphoric mountains can be hazardous to your health. It can sap your energy and weaken your resolve to endure to the top. As mountaineers must be mindful of potential avalanches, crevasses, high winds, falling rocks, and storms, researchers, too, must be aware of the dissertation hazards along their path. These hazards can hinder progress in completing your dissertation.

Dissertating is not just an intellectual endeavor but also a psychological one, to which most graduates will attest. It is truly a personal pilgrimage—one that tests your stamina, self-confidence, and emotional resilience. The only way you will ever become a doctor is to willingly struggle against the obstacles that get in your way and to do so without quitting. Be forewarned. You will want to quit, but quitting and wanting to quit are very different things. The inner resources you bring to the task keep you on the path. These inner resources are discussed later in this chapter.

Being aware of the hazards of dissertating helps you select suitable routes and make adjustments to overcome the risks. Make no mistake, dissertating is high-altitude climbing! Three hazards of this high-altitude climbing that you should be aware of are procrastination, emotional barriers, and writer's block. The next sections describe these hazards and provide some strategies for dealing with them.

Procrastination

To *procrastinate* means to put off intentionally and habitually doing something that should be done. It is a habit that steals away some of life's greatest opportunities, yet it is a habit most of us possess. Many books deal with overcoming procrastination, yet we seem to either put off reading them or fail to heed their advice. This habit, quite common among dissertation students, can result in an ABD (all-but-dissertation) status rather than an EdD or PhD. This amounts to aborting the climb to the peak and settling for heartbreak hill. I am acutely aware of the whole complex of dazzling excuses proffered by dissertation writers. With my doctoral students, I found that dissertation avoidance is often elevated to an elegant art form. Certainly, there are occasionally excellent reasons for putting off working on your dissertation. Emergencies, interruptions from others, and acts of God happen to all of us from time to time. However, the students I worry about are those who keep themselves from starting or continuing because they fear the unknown, lack the self-confidence to move ahead on their own, or engage in irrational thinking, such as awfulizing. They convince themselves the task is awful, horrible, and unbearable. But putting it off only postpones the inevitable. It is critical that you learn to recognize those signs that indicate you are putting off working.

> Putting off an easy thing makes it hard, and putting off a hard one makes it impossible.
>
> —George H. Lonmer

There are two physical laws that apply equally well to people and objects with regard to the habit of procrastination. They are Newton's law of inertia and Parkinson's Law.

You and the Law of Inertia

The law of inertia states the following: A body in motion tends to stay in motion; a body at rest tends to stay at rest. In other words, it takes greater force to get a body moving than it does to keep it moving, and when it gets moving, it takes less force to keep it moving than to stop it. Physical inertia is regulated by outside forces, but the real changes in our life's attitudes and habits come from within. As William James said, "The greatest discovery of my generation is that a person can alter his life by altering his attitude of mind." Those who succeed do so because when they head toward a specific destination, they keep going until they reach it. It's hard to stop them.

People who procrastinate find many excuses for not moving up the mountain. Certainly, some excuses are quite legitimate—a family or health crisis, and so on. But you cannot be productive if you allow yourself to procrastinate for long periods of time. To overcome inertia, you must get started and build momentum. Decide to do it now. Once you realize that inertia is a normal part of our human experience, it is easier to deal with.

A habit develops when you take action so many times that it becomes automatic. How does one break the procrastination habit? I found that the best way is to develop the reverse habit—refuse to procrastinate. If you refuse to procrastinate often enough, then that also becomes a habitual response. Here are some strategies to help reverse the habit of procrastination.

1. Challenge Your Excuses

Through the years, I witnessed a variety of creative excuses offered by doctoral students to themselves and to me, their advisor. If you don't challenge the excuses you use, you may remain in stationary inertia, unable to make the forward progress you desire. One common excuse is that "I haven't read enough to write yet." Argue with yourself that writing helps clarify your thinking, and besides, first drafts don't have to be perfect. First drafts are first drafts; they are always improved with rereading. If one of your excuses is that you "need deadlines to work effectively," argue with yourself that waiting until the deadline to get started results in undue stress and leaves you tired, uncreative, and irritable. It can also affect the quality of your writing. Conducting inner debates about any "logical" excuse keeps you from stalling.

EXERCISE

Here is an excellent exercise to help you learn about your excuses. It was developed by Stan Hibbs (drhibbs@drhibbs.com) and reprinted in the All-But-Dissertation Survival Guide located at www.ecoach.com. He asks that you write out every excuse you make for not working on your dissertation. Then write a rebuttal for each excuse. He gives the following examples:

(Continued)

(Continued)

Excuse: I don't have time.

Rebuttal: My time is limited, but I can always get started and get something done. I'll feel so much better if I do.

Excuse: I'm just not up to it today.

Rebuttal: I don't feel very excited about working on it today, but I'll feel great if I make some progress.

Excuse: I've got a lot of errands to run.

Rebuttal: Yes, there are some things I could do, but that's not going to get me my doctorate. I'll go on the errands after I make some progress today.

Once the rebuttal list is complete, write each one down on a separate 3" × 5" index card. Carry these cards with you to use as flash cards to memorize your rebuttals. It's much harder to procrastinate when your excuses don't work anymore.

2. Develop a Do It Now! Habit

This self-motivator was recommended by W. Clement Stone (1962) in *The Success System That Never Fails*. He claimed it sparks you to action. Here's what you do: Repeat *Do it now!* to yourself 50 times or more in the morning and evening, and whenever it occurs to you throughout the day. This imprints it indelibly in your subconscious. Every time you must do something you don't feel like doing and the self-starter *Do it now!* flashes in your mind—immediately *act* (p. 93).

The *Do it now!* habit also helps when you're in the dissertation gloom-and-doom state. Consider adopting Denis Waitley's (1987) personal motto, "Stop Stewing and Start Doing." He said, "I can't be depressed and active at the same time" (p. 147).

> Nothing is so fatiguing as the eternal hanging on of an uncompleted task.
>
> —William James

Another technique to acquire this self-starting habit is to post a sign that says *Do it now!* around your house and desk. It helps jog your memory.

3. Divide and Conquer

Mountains are overwhelming and, in their entirety, intimidating. They can't be conquered all at once. In technical climbs, we move up the mountain in a series of pitches—one hand and toe hold at a time until we stand spent but elated on the top. Looking at the entire dissertation can also be overwhelming. Think of your dissertation as a mountain with stairs—a set of small steps leading to the top. It is important to break it down into small, achievable goals and take it step by step.

> The journey of a thousand miles begins and ends with one step.
>
> —Lao Tse

One strategy is to make a contract with yourself that states specific goals, establishes completion dates, and offers rewards for attaining your goals. It is important that you write these completion dates on your appointment calendar. There's a wonderful feeling of exhilaration that goes along with accomplishment. It gives you a new burst of energy to keep moving.

4. Remove the Reward

Procrastination should not be a pleasant experience. If you procrastinate by socializing or getting a cup of coffee, stop it! Procrastinate in unpleasant conditions. For example, lock yourself in your office—no visitors, no coffee. When the enjoyment goes away, so will your procrastination.

5. Discipline Yourself

If you really don't want to write, promise yourself you'll write for 15 minutes. Set a timer, and when it rings, decide if you will work for 15 more minutes or quit. Often the hardest part is starting. This strategy helps you build that momentum to overcome inertia.

> Dreams are what get you started. Discipline is what keeps you going.
>
> —Jim Ryan, Sportsman

You and Parkinson's Law

Parkinson's Law is a ready-made excuse. It states, "Work expands to fill the time available for its completion." This law applies especially to dissertation writers. Most doctoral candidates have families and hold full-time jobs. It is so easy for other work (job and family obligations) to fill all the available time, leaving no time to write the dissertation. Competing demands for your time are always problematic, and let's face it, immediate gratification and family fun are more seductive than confronting your dissertation mountain.

So how do you overcome Parkinson's Law? Invoke the Premack principle. The Premack principle, often called *grandma's rule*, states that a high-frequency activity can be used to reinforce low-frequency behavior. Access to the preferred activity is contingent on completing the low-frequency behavior. Grandma knew this simply as, "Before you can watch TV, you have to help with the dishes." This is a simple behavioral principle behind the "work first, play second" maxim. What is it you most like to do? Surf the Internet? Watch TV? Shop? Complete a dissertation task, then do something you really enjoy. For example, "Before I can watch TV, I have to revise my questionnaire." Or "If I complete Chapter 1, I can see a movie on the weekend." Disciplining yourself in this way keeps you on task and keeps your momentum in high gear. You will complete your dissertation in record time.

> The best way to break a habit is to drop it.
>
> —Leo Aikman

Emotional Barriers

Students often describe their experience of writing the dissertation as a roller-coaster ride, with definite ups and downs associated with each phase of the process. They refer to the down times as the *dissertation doldrums*, where they feel discouraged, depressed, frustrated, and anxious. They even doubt their ability to complete the project. These feelings are predictable for anyone trying to achieve a high goal; however, these negative emotions can easily overpower you. If you don't address them, they will immobilize you, sap your energy, and keep you from achieving your goal. When things go well, you are elated and you soar on cloud nine. These feelings of exhilaration provide the momentum to "keep on keeping on." The ups and downs of dissertating—the pains and the joys—are experienced by all writers. It's part of the dissertation process and to be expected. Here are some strategies to help you deal with the dissertation doldrums:

1. Reflect on Your Reasons for Obtaining Your Doctorate

Sometimes you question your own sanity for undertaking this massive project. You wonder why you continue to torture yourself in this way. When you have these feelings, take time to reflect on the reasons you decided to enroll in a doctoral program. More than likely, they are still valid and should serve to reinforce your commitment and motivation to stay on track. Take time to reflect on these reasons, write them down, and visualize your life after graduation and a title after your name.

2. Establish a Support Committee

When the going gets rough, you may reach an impasse in your progress. That's when you assemble a support committee—those who believe in you and have your best interests at heart—friends, mentors, and family members. You might ask your mother to chair this committee. These are your cheerleaders and confidants when you're down; they share your joys and bad days and provide regular pep talks to overcome your discouragement. They also let you know when you are indulging yourself in complaining and offer you encouragement rather than pampering.

Writer's Block

All dissertation writers experience writer's block at some point during the process. It's that longing to be anywhere but in front of the computer. When this happens, everything else in your life takes priority over writing. Taking the dog for a walk, cleaning your closets, running errands, washing clothes, and e-mailing friends appear crucial. Writer's block can be caused by any number of factors: lack of confidence, fear, time constraints, no outline, personal issues, frustration with your topic, perfectionism, weariness. It is important to identify the obstacles that stifle your writing. In other words, take time to fall back and regroup. Unfortunately, there is no magic formula to keep you in the writing groove, but here are some strategies that might help you keep the words flowing.

1. Change the Mode of Putting Down Words

If you're stuck on the computer, try a dictation machine or writing by hand, or change where you write—go outside, to a friendly coffee shop, or to the library.

2. Get Some Physical Exercise

Get outside and walk; mow the lawn. Physical activity of the pleasant and slightly mindless kind can precipitate creative thinking.

3. Make Two Lists

This exercise helps you get a handle on the root of your block. Whenever you are trying to write your dissertation but find yourself blank-minded and wordless, write two lists labeled as follows:

1. I ought to write X because . . .

2. I refuse to write X because . . .

The second list will be more informative than the first in that it brings to your conscious mind the refusals that may be lying at the subconscious level. You can then take steps to overcome your refusals.

4. Cluster Your Ideas

This is the old psychology game where one person says a word and the second person responds immediately with the very next word that comes to mind. First, write your subject on paper and circle it. Then, write down the very next thing you think of and circle that. Draw a line connecting these two circles. Next, write down what you thought of as you wrote the second word and draw a line connecting it to the previous word. Follow this process until you have exhausted your brain! Write down everything that comes to your mind no matter how far out. After you complete the entire process, you will be amazed at the words that popped out.

A similar method that works for my students is to cluster ideas using sticky notes. In the center of a large poster-size paper, write your subject and surround it with large circles. Then write all ideas connected with the subject on sticky notes and place them inside the circles. If desired, you can then use extra-small colored tags to add ideas to the larger notes. The beauty of this method is that you can move the sticky notes around as necessary. This mind-storming technique works well with groups working together. It allows individuals to build on ideas generated by others, thereby obtaining a broader perspective on the subject.

5. Write a Crummy First Draft

Perfectionists cringe at this thought. Just know that no one, however gifted, can write an acceptable first draft.

You don't have to write something *good* initially. Thinking that you do only causes self-disparagement and self-recrimination. Remember, first drafts are only *first* drafts and are for your eyes only. Let them be sketchy thoughts, rambling sentences, clumsy word patterns using poor grammar, and so on. Just get everything out of your brain and onto paper. Don't obsess and ponder ideas too long. Don't judge it, just *write it*. Getting your ideas on paper gets you moving. You now have something to work on and revise. Accept the fact that you will be writing several drafts, and take the pressure off the first one by concentrating only on your ideas. Most writers agree that it's easier to revise than to create. Writing is a complex and slow process, so don't expect it to flow effortlessly. Few writers write only when they feel inspired. If you wait for inspiration, or write only when you feel like it, your chances of completion are nil.

Although all of the preceding suggestions are useful, over time you will work out your own best ways and means for moving on.

What Are the Inner Essentials?

The Backpack "Ten Essentials"

To keep any climb safe and enjoyable, preparation and good judgment are critical. Just as it's important that mountaineers recognize the awesome powers of nature for which they must be prepared, so must you understand the immenseness and complexity of the dissertation task and be prepared for it. Experienced mountaineers rely on a time-tested packing list, known as the "Ten Essentials," developed in the 1930s by a group of Seattle-area climbing enthusiasts. The Ten Essentials are what every outdoor person should carry at all times in his or her backpack to ensure survival. They include a map, compass, flashlight, extra food, extra clothing, sunglasses, first-aid kit, pocketknife, a fire starter, and water. The list is often expanded as the need arises.

These were mandatory items in my backpack when I trained for my Basic Mountaineering Training Course certificate from the Sierra Club. When the unexpected happened on mountain trails, I realized how truly essential they are. Climbing the dissertation mountain requires the presence of certain inner essentials to make it safely and successfully to the top. Inner resources are those intangible reserves that help you cope with problems and crises. Especially in times of stress, it is the mobilization of these noteworthy attributes that helps remove or transcend the barriers you face along the path. In the words of German philosopher Friedrich Nietzsche, "That which does not kill me, makes me stronger."

The Dissertation Journey's "Essentials"

The dissertation journey requires innumerable inner essentials. Some of the dissertation writer's essentials are commitment, perseverance, stamina, positive mental attitude, courage, and the spirit of adventure. Although these six essentials are not the only ones, they are vital to your survival and ultimate success on the journey.

Commitment

Commitment is the willingness to do whatever it takes to achieve your goal. It is one thing to start something; it is quite something else to complete it. A genuine commitment is a promise you make to yourself to stick it out regardless of the obstacles you face or how many times you are knocked down. You simply get up and press on.

> The moment you commit and quit holding back, all sorts of unforeseen incidents, meetings and material assistance will rise up to help you. The simple act of commitment is a powerful magnet for help.
>
> —Napoleon Hill

Becoming a doctor is only a dream until you commit the time and energy to obtain it. Imagine your name with a PhD or an EdD after it. Tom Flores, an NFL coach, said, "A total commitment is paramount to reaching the ultimate in performance." Making a commitment gives you that extra ounce of courage that keeps you going during the tough times. Abraham Lincoln gave this advice: "Always bear in mind that your own resolution to succeed is more important than any other thing."

Perseverance

Perseverance is that attribute that impels you to go on resolutely, in spite of obstacles, criticism, adversity, fears, or tears, to overcome the inevitable discouragement and disappointment that accompanies mountainous-type projects. It means putting in the hard work necessary to get the job done, even when you don't want to. Having

> Nothing in the world can take the place of persistence. Talent will not... genius will not... education will not.... Persistence and determination alone are omnipotent.
>
> —Calvin Coolidge

spent long, relentless hours of effort over a long period of time, it's easy to lose heart and want to quit. This is when you dig deep into your inner reserves and keep going. Remember there is a big difference between quitting and wanting to quit. The difference is between being ABD (all-but-dissertation) and becoming a doctor. High achievement is not reserved for those with innate talent or high IQs. It is dependent on desire and perseverance—on that extra effort. Students start their doctoral program expecting to be successful, but only those who are willing to pay the price and do what's required finish. There's an old saying, "A big shot is only a little shot who kept shooting."

Stamina

High-altitude climbing takes a tremendous amount of energy. It involves continual exertion and makes brutal demands on your legs, lungs, and heart. *Stamina* is what it takes! It's not optional. Writing a dissertation requires stamina—the strength to sustain long hours of work and yet maintain high performance. This is especially difficult when juggling the demands of a full-time job and sustaining family obligations while completing a doctorate. However, stamina is essential to surviving the journey.

Lessons from athletes can be of great value. For example, athletes learn to focus and trigger the relaxation response through deep and steady breathing techniques. Meditation and visualization techniques are extremely valuable in managing stress. You can get a second wind by taking time to refresh and rest your brain and body. Regular exercise also rejuvenates the mind and body and reduces stress. Good nutrition and a good night's rest are also vital to maintaining stamina. Staying emotionally healthy is easier if you are in good shape physically.

Positive Mental Attitude

A significant psychological discovery in the past 20 years is that people can choose the way they think. Henry Ford put it this way, "Whether you think you can or can't, you're right." A *positive mental attitude* is at the core of any high achievement and success in life. Try to avoid negative thoughts or negative self-talk whenever possible. These include thoughts such as "I don't have time now so it's not worth starting" or "This will be too hard." It also helps to remove from your vocabulary words like *can't, never,* or *awful.* They only keep you on a downward spiral. One technique that works when you hear yourself being negative is to say *Stop!* Stopping these negative thoughts interrupts the downward spiral.

> Everything can be taken from man except the last of the human freedoms, his ability to choose his own attitude in any given set of circumstances—to choose his own way.
>
> —Victor Frankl

I know many doctoral students who focus on the difficulties, the unpleasant times, and the pains associated with struggling. Thus, they create for themselves a miserable experience. The students I know who possess a positive mental attitude look for the good in situations, even when it's hard to find. Their optimism is like a beacon that propels them forward, thus creating a joyful experience for them.

Courage

It takes *courage* to face the fears and doubts that often accompany writing a dissertation. During the first class of the research sequence at the university where I teach, I ask my students to describe the greatest fears and anxieties they have about the dissertation process.

Their responses run the gamut from reasonable to unreasonable. Here are the most commonly identified fears and anxieties:

- The negative impact on work and family
- Not measuring up to the task intellectually
- Lack of the necessary research skills
- Not enough time to do everything that needs to be done
- Fear of the unknown—don't know what they don't know
- Won't find an appropriate topic or an advisor
- Being overwhelmed
- Fear of criticism and committee rejections of their work
- Fear of failure
- Being emotionally vulnerable

These fears cause considerable anxiety at times, which can result in self-doubt, insecurity, worry, and procrastination that keep you from doing your best work and moving forward. I found that sharing these fears and anxieties with others lessens their impact and helps you realize that everyone involved in the dissertation process has at least one or more of the same vulnerabilities. Facing them openly and honestly goes a long way toward bringing out the courage that sustains the most fearful.

> Courage is the mastery of fear, not the absence of fear.
>
> —Mark Twain

Spirit of Adventure

Adventure is defined as (1) an undertaking usually involving danger and unknown risks and (2) an exciting or remarkable experience. The spirit of adventure means accepting a risk and standing up to your fear of the unknown—taking the path less traveled. The central motivation for adventuring is to attempt something you're not sure can be done, to go somewhere you're not sure you can go.

If you know what you want, why you want it, and are willing to sacrifice and endure many obstacles to get it, then you have the true spirit of adventure. It's all about being willing to explore your own limits. Whether it's a physical adventure or a mental one, it is always replete with excitement, hazards, and triumphs along the way. Are you comfortable with ambiguity? Climbers must risk and face uncertainty. If you believe your journey to become a doctor is an adventure filled with new learnings and discoveries about yourself,

> Whatever you dream you can do, begin it. Boldness has genius, power and magic.
>
> —Goethe

others, and your field of interest, your life will be transformed, and you will contribute significantly to your world.

Summary

This first chapter helped you understand the dissertation journey as a peak experience, a transformative and fulfilling life event. Completing the journey successfully requires understanding the sacrifices, stresses, and uncertainties you face along the path. It also requires knowing strategies to deal with the major hazards facing dissertation writers: procrastination, emotional barriers, and writer's block.

Climbing the dissertation mountain safely and successfully requires inner essentials such as commitment, perseverance, stamina, a positive mental attitude, courage, and a spirit of adventure. Commitment is the promise you make to yourself to complete the dissertation regardless of the obstacles you face along the way. Perseverance means staying the course even when you don't want to. Stamina requires the ability to sustain long hours of work while juggling work and family obligations and still achieving your goal. A positive mental attitude makes the difference between experiencing misery or joy along the path. Courage overcomes fear and self-doubt. A spirit of adventure means a willingness to explore your own limits and view the dissertation journey as a quest filled with new learnings and discoveries.

The next chapter familiarizes you with the mountain's terrain—the dissertation document itself. You learn about the dissertation's structure, format, typical components, major steps in the process, and individual's roles and responsibilities.

2

What Exactly Is a Dissertation?

Any successful mountain climb, whether actual or metaphorical, requires knowledge of the terrain and the environment. The more knowledge, the better the chance of success. No mountaineer would begin a major ascent without a solid understanding of the unique nature of the mountain, its challenges, characteristics, and vagaries. So, too, must a dissertation writer fully understand the nature of the doctoral dissertation. This chapter describes the essence of the dissertation—its component parts, major steps in the dissertation process, and the roles and responsibilities of those involved.

What Is a Doctoral Dissertation?

A doctoral dissertation is a formal document that demonstrates your ability to conduct research that makes an original contribution to theory or practice. It is a partial fulfillment of the requirements for an EdD or PhD degree. The term *original,* according to the Council of Graduate Schools (2002), "implies some novel twist, fresh perspective, new hypothesis, or innovative method that makes the dissertation project a distinctive contribution" (p. 10).

The dissertation requirement is viewed differently in programs leading to applied degrees, such as the EdD, DPA, and PsyD, than it is in those awarding the PhD. The distinction in focus between the two is discussed in the *Handbook of Accreditation of the Western Association of Schools and Colleges* (Western Association of Schools and Colleges, 2008) as follows:

> **PhD Degrees:** The standard research-oriented degree which indicates that the recipient has done, and is prepared to do, original research in a major discipline. The PhD usually requires three years or more of postgraduate work including an original research dissertation or project.
>
> **MD, EdD, JD, etc.:** Degrees with emphasis on professional knowledge and practice. These degrees normally require three or more years of prescribed postgraduate work (p. 56).

While both types of doctorates expect original research, candidates in an applied doctoral program (e.g., EdD) focus on applied research that supports the advancement of the profession.

The dissertation document may vary in format depending on the type of study, but essentially all researchers define a problem with researchable questions, conduct an exhaustive review of the literature, choose an appropriate methodology, collect and analyze data, and present the findings and conclusions.

The length of dissertations varies dramatically. No set number of pages is required. However, if it is excessively long, readers may lose the will to live. It helps to follow the rule of thumb illustrated by this apocryphal story: A young boy, after meeting the towering Abraham Lincoln, asked the president, "How long should a man's legs be?" Lincoln answered, "Long enough to reach the ground." It's the same way with dissertations. The appropriate length depends on the degree to which you responsibly and comprehensively answer your study's research questions.

Completing a dissertation represents the pinnacle of academic achievement. It requires high-level skills of discernment and critical analysis, proficiency in at least one research method, and the ability to communicate the results of that research in a clear, coherent, and concise manner. No previous writing experiences prepare you for such a challenging and rigorous task. Basically, it's a learn-and-grow-as-you-go process.

One efficient way to learn the dissertation terrain is to familiarize yourself with dissertations previously published in your chosen field of study. This helps you understand the format and style of accepted dissertations. Also read dissertations chaired by those individuals you are considering for advisors. This way you can obtain insight into that person's expectations and level of scholarship.

Typical Dissertation Structure

A dissertation's structure varies with the academic discipline and the methodology used. Chapter names may be different, but in one way or another, the questions displayed as follows are answered. Figure 2.1 is an overview of a typical dissertation's basic structure.

Most researchers try to resolve a specific problem and advance learning by answering the questions posed in Figure 2.1. Regardless of academic discipline, research usually follows the scientific method and has the same basic format, with some variations. To conceptualize your study, determine what the overall format will be. I ask my students to create a loose-leaf notebook with tabs depicting the dissertation's major sections. The notebook serves as an outline for the entire study. As students write individual sections, they insert them into the notebook.

Figure 2.1 Typical Dissertation Structure

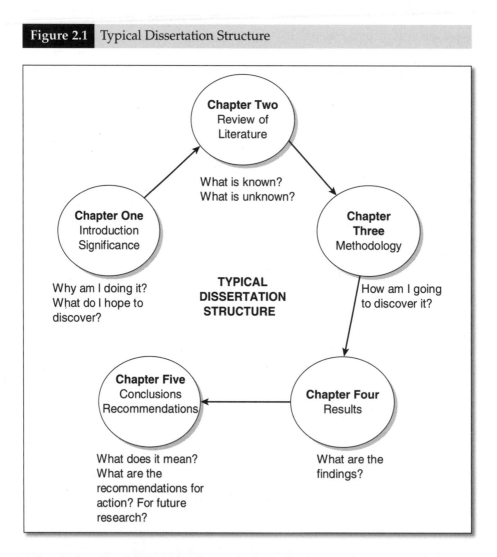

Following are sample formats of studies using quantitative and qualitative methodologies and some alternative formats. A quantitative study generally adheres to a rigid standard found in research studies, although the order of the various sections may vary.

Studies Using Quantitative Methodology: Sample Format

Chapter 1	Introduction/problem statement
	Purpose of the study
	Research questions/hypotheses
	Significance of the study
	Delimitations/assumptions
	Definition of terms
Chapter 2	Literature review
Chapter 3	Methodology
	Kind of research
	Population and sample
	Instrumentation
	Data collection procedures
	Statistical analysis procedures
Chapter 4	Limitations
	Results
	Findings
Chapter 5	Summary
	Conclusions, implications, recommendations

Studies using qualitative methodology are much less standardized than quantitative studies. However, they should be consistent with the assumptions inherent in the qualitative approach.

Studies Using Qualitative Methodology: Sample Format

Chapter 1	Introduction
	Conceptual framework
	Topic and research problem
	Rationale/purpose of the study
	Guiding questions
	Significance of the study
	Delimitations
Chapter 2	Review of the literature

Chapter 3   Methodology

Rationale and assumptions for the qualitative design

Type of design

Researcher's role

Site and sample selections

Data collection techniques

Managing and recording data

Data analysis procedures

Chapter 4   Methods for verification/trustworthiness

Chapter 5   Limitations

Results/outcome of the study

Discussion

Connections to previous research and theories

Conclusions

Implications

Suggestions for future research

Alternative Formats

Model-Building Studies

Chapter 1   Problem and purpose

Chapter 2   Literature review

Chapter 3   Methodology

Chapter 4   Analysis of data

Chapter 5   Conclusion and model

Case Studies

Chapter 1   Problem and purpose

Chapter 2   Literature review

Chapter 3   Methodology

Chapters 4–6   Case studies

Chapter 7   Analysis of themes

Chapter 8   Conclusions, implications, and recommendations

Components of a Typical Dissertation

Title Page

The title page, the first page of your dissertation, includes the title, author, the degree requirements that the dissertation fulfills, and the date. The title of the dissertation is a succinct summary of the topic and generally should not exceed 15 words. Avoid unnecessary words, such as "A Study of . . ." The title includes key terms that readily identify the scope and nature of your study.

Copyright Page

Copyrighting the dissertation, although highly desirable, is optional. It is not required that you formally register your dissertation with the U.S. Copyright Office in order to obtain copyright protection, but it is highly desirable to do so in case of any copyright litigation. Regardless of whether you formally register with the U.S. Copyright Office, a notice of copyright should appear on the page immediately following the title page. This informs others that your dissertation is not available for unrestricted use.

Committee Approval Page

This page contains the date of approval and the original signatures of your dissertation committee, the outside reader (if one is appointed), and the dean. By signing this page, they attest to the fact that they have read and approved your work.

Vita and Resume

Vitas and resumes are not typically included in dissertations, but they can be. If you choose to include a vita or resume, it should be selective rather than exhaustive and should be limited to one page. Most dissertations include this at the end of the dissertation, following the references.

Abstract of the Dissertation

The abstract is a brief summary of the dissertation. The abstract should be well organized, concise, and self-contained because it is often printed separately. A copy of the abstract is frequently bound in the dissertation.

Table of Contents

The table of contents is essentially a topic outline of your dissertation, including all headings and subheadings, with accompanying page numbers. The following are generally included: acknowledgments, dedication, statement of the problem, review of the literature, methodology, analysis of the data, conclusions and recommendations, appendixes, and references. Each table of contents entry *must* correspond exactly to the title in the text. Consider preparing your table of contents ahead of time as a tentative outline for your study. It provides a good checklist for what needs to be done in writing the dissertation.

List of Figures, Illustrations, and Tables

Separate lists should be created for figures, illustrations, and tables. These lists should include the number and full name of each table, figure, or illustration as they are stated in the text. In addition, they should be listed in order of appearance in the text, followed by the number of the page on which the table, figure, or illustration appears.

Acknowledgment Page (Optional)

Acknowledgments give credit to others for their guidance and assistance throughout the dissertation process. It generally recognizes the contributions of such individuals as committee members, other significant faculty, helpful colleagues, technical consultants, typists, or family and friends. Acknowledgments may also express gratitude for the use of copyrighted or other restricted materials.

Dedication Page (Optional)

You may choose to dedicate your dissertation to a person or persons who have had a significant impact on your work. It gives you the opportunity to give special tribute to those who provided extraordinary support and encouragement. The dedication tribute may be placed at the end of the acknowledgment section, or it may be a separate section.

Chapter 1: Introduction or Problem Statement

This section of the dissertation gives you an opportunity to grab readers' attention and bring them on board with interest. It presents the problem addressed by the research, and it supplies a brief summary of the most relevant research and theory pertaining to the subject of the study. The problem statement should tell the story behind the research intent. It should provide the background to the purpose statement and research questions. In addition to the introductory problem statement, this section usually contains the purpose statement, research questions or hypotheses, the significance of the study, a definition of terms, delimitations/assumptions, and organization of the study. As an option, a brief summary of the introduction may appear at the end of the chapter. In addition, summaries may be used to conclude the subsequent chapters.

Chapter 2: Review of the Literature

The review of literature is a summation of pertinent literature directly related to your study. It provides a background for the important variables or concepts in your study and describes the similarity and difference between your work and that of other authors and researchers in the field. This review of the literature is traditionally your second chapter, but there may be reasons to include it later in the dissertation.

Chapter 3: Methodology

The methodology section describes in detail how the study was conducted. This chapter usually consists of the following sections: kind of research, sample and/or population, instrumentation, data collection procedures, data analysis, and limitations of the study.

Chapter 4: Results or Findings

This section summarizes the data collected and details the statistical treatment of those data, if any. Tables, figures, or illustrations are used to report data clearly and economically. Findings are usually summarized at the end of the chapter. A qualitative study usually consists of narrative descriptions embodied in themes and patterns generated from the data.

Chapter 5: Conclusions, Recommendations, Implications

This section describes what the findings mean and what conclusions you drew from the research questions that guided your study. It details how your findings compare with those in the literature and with your conceptual framework. Included in this chapter are practical implications for professional practice as well as recommendations for further research.

References, Endnotes, or Bibliographies

A reference section at the end of the dissertation should list all works cited in the dissertation. A bibliography includes related material that you reviewed and studied but did not cite directly in the text. This helps the reader determine the scope of the research behind your dissertation. However, it should not include every article or book you read. There are distinct formats for citing references, including endnotes, that you may use depending on your university's preference. Once a format is selected, be consistent and follow it throughout the dissertation.

Appendixes

Materials that document important components of the dissertation that would be too lengthy, awkward, or distracting to include within the text should be included as appendixes. These materials might be raw data, letters of introduction to participants, long or complex tables, and questionnaires. Such detail is useful to anyone trying to replicate your study in the future. Place items in the appendixes in the order they appear in the text. When more than one appendix is used, each must be designated by a letter (e.g., Appendix A, Appendix B) as well as by a title.

Major Steps in the Dissertation Process

Following is a brief description of the major steps needed to complete a dissertation. Procedures vary from university to university, and most universities distribute specific directions to their dissertation writers. Be sure to become familiar with these procedures as early as possible.

1. Select a Dissertation Topic

Deciding if a particular topic has the potential for becoming a dissertation is one of the biggest challenges faced by doctoral students. There are no hard-and-fast rules in selecting a topic; however, the following are some criteria that will help in making your decision:

    a. It needs to hold your interest over a long period of time.

    b. It must be manageable in size.

    c. It must have the potential to make an original and significant contribution to knowledge.

    d. It should be doable within your time frame and budget.

    e. It must be based on obtainable data.

    f. It should be of interest to an advisor or committee.

2. Prepare a Prospectus or Proposal

A prospectus is a 3- to 5-page overview of your study. It is basically a research concept paper that includes (1) background information about the topic with a brief commentary on pertinent literature, (2) a purpose statement, (3) research questions, and (4) appropriate methodology. This paper provides the basis for development of the proposal itself. It can also be used for discussions with potential dissertation advisors and committee members. Discussing your prospectus with a potential advisor or with potential committee members helps you obtain advice early in the dissertation process about the suitability of your topic as a worthwhile study and determine if the research questions and methodology are appropriate. A formal proposal expands on the prospectus and includes most of the components found in Chapter 1 and Chapter 3.

3. Select an Advisor

Spend time getting to know those individuals who are available to be your advisor or committee members. Present your prospectus/proposal to those with whom you might like to work, and get their views about the topic and proposed methodology. Once you select your advisor, you work with him or her to focus and refine your topic into a manageable study.

4. Choose Committee Members

In consultation with your advisor, select your committee members. Ideally, they should possess earned doctorates from an accredited institution, be considered outstanding in their field, like your topic, and be willing to spend time reviewing your dissertation document.

5. Complete and Defend the Proposal

The proposal is usually written in several drafts in response to feedback from committee members. An acceptable proposal varies according to university guidelines and expectations. At my university, an acceptable proposal consists of a solid Chapter 1 and Chapter 3, either an outline or a full Chapter 2, the proposed research instrument(s) to be used in the study, and a bibliography. Whether or not the proposal is written in the future or past tense depends on the preference of your advisor. Writing it in the past tense, however, keeps you from having to adjust the tense when transitioning to the dissertation document itself. Generally, when all committee suggestions have been incorporated and your advisor concurs, a formal proposal meeting may be held. In most instances, approval of your proposal becomes a contract between you and your committee. You are to satisfactorily conduct the study as described in the proposal, and the committee signs off on the proposal.

6. Conduct the Research

In this phase of the dissertation, you refine your instrument(s) per the recommendations of the committee and conduct a pilot test to determine reliability and validity. You collect, analyze, and interpret your data.

7. Write the Dissertation

The dissertation requires a high level of scholarly writing. You must be able to express yourself logically, clearly, and precisely. If you have difficulty with academic writing, consider hiring an editor. This can save you considerable time and make life easier for your committee by lessening the number of revisions needed. It enables your committee's comments to be directed toward substance rather than style. Editorial assistance for a dissertation is usually encouraged, but *only in matters of style, not content.*

8. Schedule the Oral Defense

Your advisor typically leads the oral defense meeting in which you present and defend your dissertation in the presence of the committee and other individuals permitted by your university. An oral defense is usually considered a public meeting. At most universities, following the oral defense, the committee certifies that the candidate has

a. Passed with no revisions needed

b. Passed with minor revisions

c. Passed with major revisions

d. Not passed, yet, defense to be continued

e. Failed

9. Make Corrections and Resubmit the Dissertation

Incorporate all the changes resulting from input provided at the oral defense. Then, follow the special procedures outlined at your university.

10. Graduate and Become a Doctor!

Roles and Responsibilities

Doctoral Candidate. A doctoral candidate is usually defined as a student formally advanced to candidacy and deemed ready to start a dissertation study. It is the responsibility of the candidate to work with his or her advisor to select appropriate, qualified individuals to serve on the dissertation committee and to initiate dialogue with committee members, to follow recommended timetables, and to attend committee meetings in accordance with your advisor. It is also the candidate's responsibility to get all forms signed in proper sequence and to submit them to the appropriate individuals.

Dissertation Advisor. The dissertation advisor is the doctoral candidate's primary advisor during all phases of the dissertation process. The advisor is the leader of the dissertation committee and usually conducts both the proposal and oral defense meetings. In conjunction with other committee members, the advisor is responsible for providing technical and content advice and assistance.

Dissertation Committee. Usually, individuals who hold earned doctoral degrees from an accredited institution are invited to serve as members of the dissertation committee. The dissertation committee generally has three to five members, including the advisor. The committee's role is to provide different lenses through which to view your work. It is an opportunity to broaden your perspective by seeing your study from various vantage points. Candidates first select the dissertation advisor and, in consultation with him or her, select the other committee members. It is recommended that committee members reflect the range of expertise pertinent to the topic under study and the methodology likely to be used. Committee members are called on to advise the candidate throughout the process in areas appropriate to their expertise and interests. They also comment on written materials developed by the doctoral candidate. Committee members are responsible for evaluating and approving the proposal and the completed dissertation.

Human Subjects Review Committee. This committee is composed of a group of faculty members who review each research proposal for the purpose of safeguarding the rights and anonymity of human subjects used for research purposes.

There are a variety of different roles within each university related to the dissertation process. One important role is played by the department that processes the dissertation forms and makes sure that appropriate procedures are followed. Also, there may be university reviewers responsible for editing and reviewing the dissertation document for the proper style format.

Summary

The doctoral dissertation is a formal document that demonstrates your ability to conduct original research that contributes to theory or practice. Although variations exist, typical dissertations consist of chapters that provide background to the topic, a literature review, a description of the methodology, findings, conclusions, and recommendations for action and future research. Major steps in the dissertation process include selecting a topic, preparing a prospectus, selecting an advisor and committee members, completing and defending a proposal, conducting the research, writing the dissertation, participating in the oral defense, making corrections, and graduating.

Now that you know the dissertation terrain, it's time to consider the ethical considerations in research. It is vital to be aware of the variety of ethical issues that arise in all phases of the dissertation process. The next chapter describes ethical issues such as the rights of human subjects, the ethics of data collection and analysis, reporting findings, writing up research, and copyright law.

3

What Are the Ethical Considerations in Research?

Research ethics is a very challenging subject which the research candidate has to face, and which if not addressed correctly may cause the result of the research work to be considered tainted or even invalid.

—Remenyi et al., 1998, p. 115

Ethical issues arise in all aspects of conducting research. Such areas include attention to human rights, data collection, data analysis and interpretation, respect for the research site, writing, and disseminating the research. This section will describe some of these central issues that you should anticipate in designing your dissertation study.

What is considered ethical varies from person to person and from institution to institution. However, most professional organizations and the various disciplines within the social sciences have established their own standards or codes of ethics to guide their research activities. These guidelines, according to Rossman and Rallis (1998), "serve as standards for the ethical practice of research and are based on moral principles such as utilitarianism (the greatest good for the greatest number), theories of individual rights (the rights of the individual may supersede the interests of the greatest number), and theories of justice (fairness and equity)" (pp. 48–49). Following are some examples of professional ethical guidelines and the websites where they can be found:

- The American Psychological Association's *Ethical Principles of Psychologists and Code of Conduct,* www.apa.org/ethics/code .html
- The American Educational Research Association Ethical Standards, www.aera.net/AboutAERA/Default.aspx?menu_id=90&id=717
- The American Sociological Association Code of Ethics, www2 .asanet.org/members/ecoderev.html
- The American Anthropological Association's Code of Ethics, www.aaanet.org/committees/ethics/ethcode.htm

The following website offers a full listing of guidelines and codes of ethics for those in the social sciences: www.bc.edu/research/meta-elements/ htm/social_sciences.htm.

Institutional Review Boards

Colleges, universities, and other research institutions have institutional review boards (IRBs) whose members review proposals and approve all research conducted at their institutions. Their main purpose is the protection of those participating in a research study, particularly around ethical issues such as informed consent, protection from harm, and confidentiality. Specifically, the IRB committee's role is to protect participants from "stress, discomfort, embarrassment, invasion of privacy or potential threat to reputation" (Madsen, 1992, p. 80).

If you decide to use questionnaires or conduct interviews, experiments, or observations, you need to submit a proposal to use human subjects to the IRB before actually conducting your study. Each institution has its own procedures as to when and how proposals should be submitted to the committee. Because your dissertation committee members may request changes in your original proposal, it would behoove you to wait until after your proposal has been formally approved by your committee to approach the IRB committee. The IRB committee's signed permission is necessary before you can collect data. When submitting your proposal to the IRB, be sure to provide detailed and comprehensive information about your study, the consent process, how participants will be recruited, and how confidential information will be protected.

There are two basic types of requests made to the IRB committee: expedited review and full review. When there is minimal risk to the participants, psychologically, physically, or socially, then an expedited review is appropriate. According to Rudestam and Newton (2007), there is no clear standard to judge "minimal risk." They state the following:

> The criterion of minimal risk could pertain to research involving brief questionnaires that do not address questions likely to be disturbing to the participants. Questions regarding favored sports or preferred television programs are probably not disturbing; questions regarding childhood victimization, current mental status, and alcohol or drug abuse probably are. (p. 277)

Clear ethical standards and principles exist regarding the rights of human subjects. They deal primarily with impact on the subjects, confidentiality, coercion, and consent. It is critical that you carefully think through these issues when planning your research procedures and that you become familiar with your institution's policies and procedures in these matters. The ethical issues involved in using human subjects in research are described in the section that follows.

Rights of Human Subjects

The following rights must be granted to all participants in a research study.

Informed Consent

All prospective participants must be fully informed about the procedures and risks involved in the research project before they agree to take part. In addition, the principles of freedom and autonomy allow individuals to refuse to participate in the study or to withdraw at any time with no recriminations. In other words, their participation must be voluntary. Following are the basic elements of informed consent that must be provided to each participant:

BASIC ELEMENTS OF INFORMED CONSENT

In seeking informed consent, the following information shall be provided to each subject:

1. A statement that the study involves research, an explanation of the purposes of the research and the expected duration of the subject's participation, a description of the procedures to be followed, and identification of any procedures which are experimental;

(Continued)

(Continued)

2. A description of any reasonably foreseeable risks or discomforts to the subject;

3. A description of any benefits to the subject or to others which may reasonably be expected from the research;

4. A disclosure of appropriate alternative procedures or courses of treatment, if any, that might be advantageous to the subject;

5. A statement describing the extent, if any, to which confidentiality of records identifying the subject will be maintained;

6. For research involving more than minimal risk, an explanation as to whether any compensation and an explanation as to whether any medical treatments are available if injury occurs and, if so, what they consist of, or where further information may be obtained;

7. An explanation of whom to contact for answers to pertinent questions about the research and research subjects' rights, and whom to contact in the event of a research-related injury to the subject; and

8. A statement that participation is voluntary, refusal to participate will involve no penalty or loss of benefits to which the subject is otherwise entitled, and the subject may discontinue participation at any time without penalty of loss of benefits to which the subject is otherwise entitled.

SOURCE: United States Department of Health and Human Services, Code of Federal Regulations (45 CFR 46.116(a), pages 14–15.

It is important to note that not all studies require informed consent. Rudestam and Newton (2007) pointed out that methodologies such as "secondary analysis of data, archival research, and the systematic observation of publicly observable data, such as shoppers in a suburban mall" may require only "expedited review" due to their classification of "minimal risk" (p. 276).

Confidentiality

Assuring confidentiality is a primary responsibility of all researchers. The term *confidentiality*, according to Sieber (1992), "refers to agreements with persons about what may be done with their data" (p. 52). It refers to the identity of individual participants and to the information from participants. All participants in a research study must be informed about what happens to the data collected from them or about them and be assured that all data will be held in confidence. Individual names should not be used in any publication about the research study. Once a study's data have been collected, no one other than the researcher should have access to it. Some statistical tests require pairing up participants' pretest with posttest scores, which presents a potential problem for confidentiality. In this case, it is appropriate to assign each participant a number or code that enables you to link the pretest and posttest scores. In addition, electronic and paper files that contain the participants' confidential data should be locked and stored in a place away from public access.

Oftentimes anonymity is requested, which means there are no identifiers that indicate which individuals or organizations supplied the data. One technique used by researchers, when questionnaires are used to gather data, is to combine the data so that individual responses are subsumed under the total aggregated data. Another technique is to use fictional names to ensure anonymity.

Specific strategies researchers can use to ensure anonymity in a consent letter to participants were offered by Joan Sieber (1992) in her book, *Planning Ethically Responsible Research:*

To protect your privacy, the following measures will ensure that others do not learn your identity or what you tell me.

1. No names will be used in transcribing from the audio tape or in writing up the case study. Each person will be assigned a letter name as follows: M for mother, F for father, MSI for male first sibling, and so on.

2. All identifying characteristics, such as occupation, city, and ethnic background will be changed.

3. The audio tapes will be reviewed only in my home (and in the office of my thesis adviser).

4. The tapes and notes will be destroyed after my report of this research has been accepted for publication (or in the case of an unpublished thesis—after my thesis has been accepted by the university) . . .

(Sieber, 1992, p. 52)

In addition to issues relating to informed consent and confidentiality, ethical considerations must also be taken into account around the methodological principles and procedures undergirding a research design. Ethical issues arise around all decision points in the research process—from the initial design planning, to collecting data, accessing a research site, writing it up, and to disseminating the results. Sensitivity to these issues and how you respond to them determines whether or not others question or trust the results from your study.

Ethical Issues in Data Collection

It is important to exercise responsibility in the processes you use to gather data for your study. In the social sciences, data are collected primarily through questionnaires, interviews, participant observations, or through an action research approach. Use of the Internet and other communication technologies to gather data also requires permission from participants. Following is a notice of implied consent used by a doctoral student to collect data using a web survey. When participants clicked on the link to his web survey, they were presented with the consent information and were advised that by continuing further, they were voluntarily agreeing to participate.

Welcome! Thank you for participating in this important research project.

All students adjust to college life in different ways. With this research, I hope to describe common thoughts, feelings, and experiences of UA students. This study involves completing a questionnaire that typically takes 10 minutes.

Completing the questionnaire automatically enters you into a random drawing to **win one of ten iPods** (valued between $80 and $150). Your participation is voluntary and your decision to complete or not complete the questionnaire will in no way affect your status or treatment at the University of Alaska. By clicking on the "next" button below, you consent to voluntarily participate in this study.

Thank you!

Student name

Title

University

Telephone

E-mail address

SOURCE: Schultz, B. (2008). *Freshmen Adjustment to College at the University of Alaska: A Descriptive, Ex Post Facto Study.* Doctoral Dissertation, University of La Verne.

Access to Research Sites

It is important that you respect the research site at all times. As Stake (1994) remarked, "Qualitative researchers are guests in the private spaces of the world. Their manners should be good and their code of ethics strict" (p. 244). The main ethical concern is the degree of sensitivity you display with the site and the interaction with the people in it. Most research sites have *gatekeepers*—people in authority who control access to the site. Examples might be a school principal, college president, a company's manager, or the IRB. From them, you must ask for and obtain permission to conduct your study at their site.

Gatekeepers have concerns about the impact of your study on their organization as well as the possible disclosure of confidential information outside the organization. It is, therefore, your ethical responsibility to fully inform them about ways your study may affect the work of the organization and its members. You should also disclose ways the results of your study would benefit the organization. Through collaboration with these gatekeepers, you select those from whom you will collect data and under what circumstances.

Respecting research sites involves disturbing the everyday life and flow of activities as little as possible. Creswell (2005) suggested that participants be reminded "a day or two before data collection of the exact time and day when you will observe or interview them. Stage the data collection so that they will feel comfortable responding, and schedule it at a time that is most convenient for their schedules" (p. 225).

It is important to remember that gatekeepers have a vested interest in protecting their sites. For example, findings could have political consequences; thus, Sieber (1992) advised us to be aware that

> gatekeepers and those they serve are not always interested in objectivity. They would not want the researcher to discover something that would be damaging to them or to their organization. They may even pressure the researcher to produce results that make them look good; hence, the researcher must be careful not to enter into unethical agreements with gatekeepers. (p. 85)

Your awareness and sensitivity to gatekeepers concerns before conducting research on their sites will help you appropriately address them.

Recording Data

Audio and video recording raise significant ethical issues during data collection. To obtain greater accuracy, today's researchers almost always record unstructured or semistructured interviews. First and foremost, obtain permission from the participants and explain why you wish to audio or video record the interview or observation. In addition, explain how the recordings will be used and how they will be stored and ultimately destroyed following data transcription. Also, assure confidentiality by using fictitious names or codes.

Paul Oliver (2008), in his book *The Student's Guide to Research Ethics*, offered a strategy for relaxing participants during audio recording. He recommended that the researcher "place the tape or disc recorder within easy reach of the interviewee, and explain to them before the interview starts that they may use the pause button at any time . . . to consider their response to a particular question . . . or to reflect" (p. 46). He further stated that participants could stop the recording if they wished. Oliver (2008) also suggested that interviewees be given the opportunity to listen to the tape at the end of the session and alter their words to more accurately express their views.

Ethical Issues in Data Analysis and Interpretation

Data analysis is making sense of the data and interpreting them appropriately so as to not mislead readers. The ethical issue is not about a researcher's honest error or honest differences of data interpretation; rather, it is in regard to the intent to deceive others or misrepresent one's work. Examples of such misconduct include using inappropriate statistical techniques or other methods of measurement to enhance the significance of your research or interpreting your results in a way that supports your opinions and biases. These are ethical issues of fabrication and falsification of data.

Fabrication is making up data or results, and *falsification* is changing data or results to deliberately distort them and then including them in your research report. According to Remenyi et al. (1998), "Any attempt to window dress or manipulate and thus distort the evidence is of course unethical, as is any attempt to omit inconvenient evidence" (p. 111). Remenyi et al. (1998) also pointed out that such strategies are not useful or rational because "even when hypotheses or theoretical conjectures are rejected, the research is perfectly valid" (p. 111). It is unethical to fudge results to make your study seem more acceptable and useful; negative results still add to the body of knowledge.

In research, the accuracy of the data is paramount. Therefore, you are obliged to employ validation strategies such as triangulation, member checking, audit trail, peer debriefing, and external auditing to check the accuracy of data. For a detailed discussion of ethics and their implications for data analysis, see Chapter 11 of Miles and Huberman's (1988) book *Qualitative Data Analysis*. As an ethical researcher, it is your responsibility to be nonbiased, accurate, and honest throughout all phases of your dissertation.

Ethical Issues in Reporting Research Findings

Ethical researchers report results honestly and objectively. They don't hide negative results, engage in selective reporting, or omit conflicting data for deceptive purposes. For example, it is considered unethical to trim outliers from a data set without discussing your reasons. Roig (2006) addressed this issue by stating that

> researchers have an ethical responsibility to report the results of their studies according to their a priori plans. Any post hoc manipulations that may alter the results initially obtained, such as the elimination of outliers or the use of alternative statistical techniques, must be clearly described along with an acceptable rationale for using such techniques." (p. 35)

Another example concerns the ethics of generalizability. It is imperative that you not try to generalize the findings from your population to other populations or settings. Instead, make reference to this situation in the limitations section of your dissertation, usually found in the methodology. As an ethical researcher, it is your responsibility to accurately and honestly record and report your data using verifiable methods.

Plagiarism

Warning! Writing a dissertation that includes plagiarism can be hazardous to your career, your degree, and your reputation. Severe penalties can be levied against those who ignore the copyright law or take it lightly. Plagiarism and copyright infringement are serious matters, one of the worst academic sins.

What is plagiarism?

Plagiarism is the theft of ideas. The definition of plagiarism stated by Booth, Colomb, and Williams (1995) is the most comprehensive and helpful one that I found in the literature:

> You plagiarize when, intentionally or not, you use someone else's words or ideas but fail to credit that person. You plagiarize even when you do credit the author but use his [or her] exact words without so indicating with quotation marks or block indentation. You also plagiarize when you use words so close to those in your source, that if you placed your work next to the source, you would see that you could not have written what you did without the source at your elbow. (p. 167)

So basically, there are three ways in which you can be guilty of plagiarizing:

1. Using others' words or ideas without giving them proper credit

2. Using others' exact words without quotation marks or indentation

3. Closely paraphrasing others' words (even if citing the source)

The third way is the most challenging for doctoral students writing their dissertations. The line between paraphrasing and plagiarizing is not always clear or straightforward, and it can cause inadvertent plagiarizing of another's work.

As a researcher, you must relate findings from the literature and from other researchers, requiring that you paraphrase or quote your sources. *Paraphrasing* is simply restating in your own words what others reported and then citing the source. How closely you parallel their words, even when correctly citing the source, determines the degree to which you may be plagiarizing.

Paraphrasing does *not* mean changing a word or two in another's sentence, changing the sentence structure, or changing some words to synonyms. If you rearrange sentences in these ways, you are writing too closely to the original—which is plagiarism, not paraphrasing. Booth et al. (1995) offered a simple test to ascertain whether or not you are inadvertently plagiarizing.

> Whenever you use a source extensively, compare your page with the original. If you think someone could run her [or his] finger along your sentences and find synonyms or synonymous phrases for words in the original in roughly the same order, try again. (p. 170)

It is important to realize that words as well as ideas can be plagiarized, so be very careful when paraphrasing the work of others. If you are ever suspected of plagiarizing, it's extremely difficult to regain the trust and respect of your advisor or others who read your dissertation.

Ethics of Writing Up Research

In addition to planning and conducting ethical research, you must consider the ethics involved in writing it up. It is vital that you refrain from using biased or discriminatory language that infers inferior status to those with particular sexual orientations and lifestyles or who belong to a particular racial or ethnic group. The *APA Manual*, 6th Edition (2010) states,

"Scientific writing must be free of implied or irrelevant evaluation of the group or groups being studied" (p. 70) and offers guidelines and in-depth discussion about these issues. Rudestam and Newton (2007) also refer to the issue of bias-free writing. They advise writers to "stay current with language that is sensitive to diverse groups because what was acceptable terminology yesterday may not be acceptable today" (p. 282). To help eliminate biased language in scholarly writing, Rudestam and Newton (2007) offered the following helpful guidelines.

GUIDELINES TO HELP ELIMINATE BIAS IN SCHOLARLY WRITING

1. Substitute gender-neutral words and phrases for gender-biased words. A common mistake is the inadvertent use of sexist terms that are deeply entrenched in our culture, such as *chairman* instead of *chairperson, mothering* instead of *parenting*, and *mankind* instead of *humankind.*

2. Use designations in parallel fashion to refer to men and women equally: "5 men and 14 women," not "5 men and 14 females."

3. Do not assume that certain professions are gender related (e.g. "the scientist . . . he") and avoid sexual stereotyping (e.g., "a bright and beautiful female professor").

4. Avoid gender-biased pronouns (e.g., "A consultant may not always be able to see *his* clients"). A few nonsexist alternatives to this pervasive problem are to:

   a. Add the other gender: *"his or her* clients." This alternative should be used only occasionally because it can become very cumbersome. It is, however, preferable to awkward constructions such as *s/he, him/her,* or *he(she).*

   b. Use the plural form: "Consultants . . . *their* clients."

   c. Delete the adjective: "to see clients."

   d. Rephrase the sentence to eliminate the pronoun: "Clients may not always be seen by their consultants."

   e. Replace the masculine or feminine pronouns with *one* or *you.*

5. Do not identify people by race or ethnic group unless it is relevant. If it is relevant, try to ascertain the currently most acceptable terms and use them.

6. Avoid language that suggests evaluation or reinforces stereotypes. For example, referring to a group as "culturally deprived" is evaluative, and remarking that the "Afro-American students, not surprisingly, won the athletic events" reinforces a stereotype.

7. Don't make unsupported assumptions about various age groups (e.g., that the elderly are less intellectually able or are remarkable for continuing to work energetically). (pp. 284, 288)

Other Ethical Considerations

Copyright Law

Copyright protects original works of authorship, including both published and unpublished works. It gives the copyright owner the exclusive right to reproduce his or her work from the moment of creation up to 70 years after the author's death.

Copyright law is an extensive, complex body of law. This section is intended to provide initial information only. It is intended to help protect your dissertation from unauthorized use and to protect others' works that may be used in your dissertation. More comprehensive information is provided at the following website: www.copyright.gov.

Protection of Your Dissertation

Copyright is secured automatically when your work is created. However, to offset unauthorized use of your original work, I strongly advise that you place the copyright notice on your dissertation. Placing the copyright notice on your dissertation notifies others of your intent to protect your rights. You do not have to register your dissertation with the Library of Congress unless you wish to do so. It is not a condition of copyright protection. However, there are advantages you should be aware of, which are addressed on page 11 of the copyright website.

The form of the copyright notice consists of three elements: (1) the symbol ©, which is the letter C in a circle, the word *Copyright*, or the abbreviation *Copr.*; (2) the year of first publication of the work; and (3) the name of the copyright's owner (U.S. Copyright Office, www.copyright.gov, retrieved 2009). The elements need not appear in any particular order; however, usually they are in this order, for example:

© 2010 Carol M. Roberts

Your dissertation can be considered published as soon as it appears on the library shelf or online or is otherwise made available to the public. If you think you may want to profit from your dissertation by writing articles or a book based on your dissertation, it is important to obtain formal registration of your work. To do this, submit to the Copyright Office a fee, a form, and required copies of your dissertation. The application form can be downloaded from the following website of the U.S. Copyright Office: www.copyright.gov. This site also provides additional information about copyright basics, current fees, how to register a work, and so on.

Protection of Others' Work Used in Your Dissertation

You need not obtain permission for those works in the *public domain,* that is, works with no copyright protection or those with expired copyrights. Academic honesty, however, mandates that you acknowledge all sources used in your dissertation, even those in the public domain. If you use copyrighted material in your dissertation, you must secure permission from the owner to include it unless it falls under the doctrine of *fair use,* which allows limited reproduction of copyrighted works for educational and research purposes. This doctrine is rather complex and can have many interpretations. Miller and Taylor (1987) reported that most university style manuals permit "excerpts of up to 150 words, provided they do not constitute a major portion of the original work" (p. 46).

If you believe that what you are using falls under fair use, you need not obtain permission, but you must cite the source in footnotes or endnotes and in the references. Using copyrighted material in your dissertation without obtaining permission can be *copyright infringement* and is called *piracy* if you profit from it in any way. Both are serious infractions. Be sure to always obtain written permission from the author or publisher if you plan to use copyrighted material in your dissertation, such as tests, questionnaires, poems, figures or other artwork, or large excerpts of books. Madsen (1992) explained the process for obtaining permission:

> Send the holder of the copyright—usually the publisher of the book or article—a simple form listing the work, the pages and lines you wish to copy or quote, and the title and publisher of the work in which the material will be published. The form also should include a place for the copyright holder's signature. (p. 89)

This procedure probably will be necessary if you later decide to publish an article or write a book based on your dissertation. Should you wish to pursue more in-depth information about copyright law, refer to William S. Strong's (1998) *The Copyright Book: A Practical Guide.*

Recommended Websites

- Office of Research Integrity
  http://ori.dhhs.gov
- "Avoiding Plagiarism, Self-Plagiarism, and Other Questionable Writing Practices: A Guide to Ethical Writing" by Miguel Roig.
  http://facpub.stjohns.edu/~roigm/plagiarism/Index.html

Recommended Books

- Israel, M., & Hay, I. (2006). *Research ethics for social scientists.* Thousand Oaks, CA: Sage.
- Kimmel, A. (1988). *Ethics and values in applied social research.* Newbury Park, NJ: Sage.

Summary

Ethical issues arise in all aspects of conducting research. This chapter focused on enhancing your understanding about ethical issues such as the rights of human subjects, data collection, data analysis and interpretation, reporting research findings, plagiarism, writing up research, and other ethical considerations such as copyright law, protection of your dissertation, and protection of others' work used in your dissertation. Now it is time to prepare for the climb. The first step is to select an interesting, researchable topic to investigate. The next chapter provides some approaches to choosing your topic, where to look for potential topics, and criteria for topic selection.

PART II

Preparing for the Climb

Good fortune is what happens when opportunity meets with preparation.

—Anonymous

4

Choosing a Dissertation Topic

The first major challenge in the dissertation process lies in choosing a dissertation topic. Your choice determines how long it will take you to complete your study. For most doctoral students, it is an agonizing decision, mainly because of the uncertainty surrounding it. Has it already been adequately researched? Is it worthy of investigation? How original does it have to be? Is it manageable in scope? To know whether or not it has been researched, or if it is important to the field, you must first immerse yourself in the literature base. It would not be worthwhile to conduct another study about a problem that has been sufficiently investigated unless, however, you conduct a meta-analysis, meta-ethnographic analysis, or literature synthesis. These research approaches synthesize findings across several studies.

Approaches to Choosing a Topic

In selecting a research topic, students sometimes use what Ray Martin (1980) called "dreaming in a vacuum." He stated that some students believe great ideas come from moments of inspiration; students who walk in the park, backpack in the mountains, or sit in quiet places to contemplate learn a lot about parks, backpacking, and contemplation, but little else. Waiting for inspiration is not the best approach to topic selection. Dissertation topics do not mystically appear. Some students attempt to find a topic that fits a set of already-collected data, a certain population to which the student has access, or a preferred research methodology. This backward approach is also inappropriate and certain to irritate a potential advisor. The most effective and efficient ways to select a topic are the following:

1. Become steeped in the relevant literature.

2. Engage in discussions with faculty and other scholars in your field.

3. Write about your topic to help crystallize and organize your understanding.

Commonly, students consider three to five potential topics before finally settling on one. Scrapping a topic and starting over at least once is the norm.

Where to Look for Potential Topics

Dissertation topics rarely emerge out of the blue; you must proactively search them out. Here are some potential sources:

1. *Your own professional interests.* What excites and energizes you? What career goals could be enhanced by studying a particular topic?

2. *Faculty members, professional colleagues, and fellow students.* Listen to their suggestions about potential topics.

3. *Professional journals in your field.* This is where you can find out the hot topics of the day and for the near future.

4. *Librarians.* Ask them to help you run a database search on some topic of interest. Make a list of key words and phrases to initiate the search. The results of a computer search should help you discover whether a dissertation is possible on this topic or whether the topic has been "done to death."

5. *Dissertations.* Review previously written dissertations. Consult Proquest Dissertations and Theses *Dissertation Abstracts International* and *American Doctoral Dissertations,* from whom you can order dissertations of interest. Chapter 5 of most dissertations includes a section titled "Recommendations for Future Research." This is a gold mine of potential topics.

6. *Oral defenses.* The discussions that occur during a dissertation's oral defense often suggest potential topics. Attend as many of these as you can. It opens your eyes to what happens during a dissertation defense.

7. *Current theories.* Have any new theories come out in your field, or are existing theories being questioned?

8. *The Internet.* A variety of sources exist on the Internet.

9. *Conferences and seminars.* Often these deal with current interest areas in the field. Talk with presenters and authors to get their ideas about researchable topics.

10. *Outside agencies or professional organizations that conduct research.* Excellent resources are the 10 National Educational Regional Laboratories, www.ed.gov/EdRes/EdFed/RegLab.html, and the American Educational Research Association (AERA), http:// aera.net.

11. *Leading scholars in your interest areas.* Usually, authors and researchers eagerly talk with someone interested in their ideas and research. Call and find out what they are currently doing and ask their advice about potential studies.

12. *Your current job setting.* Are there problems that need solutions in your workplace? Your boss might have a pet topic that could enhance your career opportunities. However, be cautious. If you think a topic might be suggested in which you have no interest, you are better served not to conduct this research. A dissertation is an extensive, scholarly endeavor, and the topic should be one in which you have strong interest.

13. *References in your field.* Many handbooks and bibliographies exist in most subject areas. Some useful examples in the field of education are the following:

    a. *Handbook of Research on Teaching.* Published by the AERA, this handbook provides highly comprehensive reviews of educational research.

    b. *Harvard Educational Review.* Edited and published by graduate students at Harvard University, this journal provides reviews and opinions on the most topical educational issues.

    c. *Review of Educational Research.* Published by the AERA, this quarterly journal publishes review articles that summarize, in a comprehensive and integrated fashion, research on educational topics.

d. *Yearbook of the National Society for the Study of Education (NSSE).* Since 1902, the yearbook has published an annual volume organized around some central theme, for example, Behavior Modification in Education. Distinguished scholars in these areas write the articles. The topics are selected because of their timeliness or immediate practical value to educators and researchers (Martin, 1980, p. 7).

All discipline areas have their own encyclopedias, handbooks, or yearbooks. You can access them on the Internet by keying in your area (e.g., sociology, psychology) followed by the word *handbook, yearbook,* and so on.

Some Criteria for Topic Selection

How do you know if your particular topic has the potential to become a scholarly dissertation? Most universities and doctoral faculties agree that the doctoral dissertation should be an original piece of research and significant to the field. However, what constitutes originality or significance is open to interpretation and usually differs among various faculty advisors. Madsen (1992) clarified the elusive term *originality.* He claims that a topic must have the potential to do at least one of the following:

> Uncover new facts or principles, suggest relationships that were previously unrecognized, challenge existing truths or assumptions, afford new insights into little-understood phenomena, or suggest new interpretations of known facts that can alter people's perceptions of the world around them. (p. 38)

No hard-and-fast rules exist for selecting a topic. Ogden (1993) reminded us that "the basic purpose of a dissertation is to demonstrate that you can do acceptable research in your field. It is not your life's work" (p. 39). Following are some general criteria for considering potential topics:

1. *It needs to hold your interest for a long time.* It takes longer than you anticipate to write an acceptable dissertation.

2. *It must be manageable in size.* Most students begin with a topic that is too large. Remember you can't do it all. Your goal is to add a small but significant piece to the knowledge base and graduate! Save the Nobel Prize–level research to do as a postgraduate.

3. *It must have the potential to make an original and significant contribution to knowledge.* Can you find a hole, a gap, a missing piece in the knowledge base you can fill and would be useful to theory or practice?

4. *It must be doable within your time frame and budget.* Given your current situation, is it a feasible topic to undertake? Traveling to Russia or conducting a longitudinal study may not be possible.

5. *It has to have obtainable data.* You must be able to collect data for the study from an appropriate sample size in a reasonable period of time.

6. *It has not already been sufficiently researched.* There is no value to conducting one more study about a topic that has been researched over and over again.

7. *It should be acceptable to your advisor and committee members.* The signatures of these individuals determine whether or not you become "doctor."

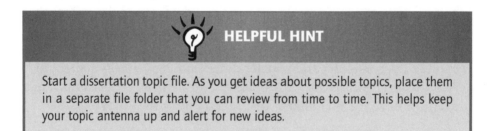

HELPFUL HINT

Start a dissertation topic file. As you get ideas about possible topics, place them in a separate file folder that you can review from time to time. This helps keep your topic antenna up and alert for new ideas.

I cannot emphasize enough the importance of making a concerted effort to become familiar with the literature and to talk with experts in your field. You cannot know for certain if the topic you desire is significant, nor can you have a clear notion about what is known and not known about the topic. Just because *you* don't know, doesn't mean it is not known.

HELPFUL HINT

- A truism: You will encounter a wide range of opinions regarding the worth of any dissertation topic. Some might think it outstanding, while others claim it has no value. Such a variety of opinions reflects each individual's particular interest, experience, or bias. The thing to remember is that you only have to satisfy your dissertation committee to pursue a topic that interests you.

- Another truism: Stubbornness in pursuing a dissertation topic no one believes worthy of research can lead to ABDism. Time spent pursuing a lost cause can cost you valuable time and make it difficult to obtain an advisor. In other words, as the adage says, if the horse dies, get off!

Replication Studies

One strategy in pursuing a dissertation topic is to replicate a previous study. Replication simply means doing the study again. Often students think repeating another's study is cheating and just an easy way out. It is quite the opposite. Knowledge accumulates incrementally through studies that build on each other over time, and replication adds strength and clarity to research findings. You can make a valuable contribution by repeating an important study.

It may be important to verify, reinforce, or contradict the results of earlier studies (Balian, 1994).

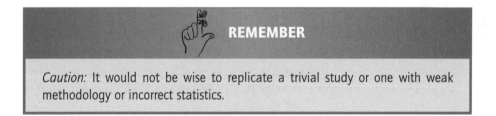

REMEMBER

Caution: It would not be wise to replicate a trivial study or one with weak methodology or incorrect statistics.

Research studies may be replicated in several ways. You might choose to alter parts of the research design of a previous study. It would also be appropriate to add or subtract variables, restate the research questions, or alter the research instrument(s). You might replicate it in a different geographic area, with a different population, or using different instrumentation (e.g., an interview instead of the original survey). These modifications, provided there is justification, can help clarify existing results.

You may adapt the research instrument(s) to fit the new population under study. However, if you use the exact instrument from the previous study, it is a "professional nicety" to ask the author's permission. You also must invent a whole new literature review. Replicating a study is not nearly as easy as it seems.

In writing the dissertation, you must state a rationale indicating why replication is important (the previous study was conducted 15 years ago, there are updated variables that may influence the results, etc.). You must also acknowledge the replication and compare your findings with previous findings.

Replication Studies Dos and Don'ts

Do	Don't
• Highlight the need to replicate • Cite replication • Contact original author for agreement (put agreement letter in appendixes) • Make it your own study • Bring a copy of the original study to your advisor • Mention the replication in your purpose statement and in your findings and interpretation chapters	• Choose a topic for convenience • Appear to be plagiarizing • Copy bibliography, literature review, or table format • Confuse adaptation with replication

Summary

Selecting an appropriate topic is one of the most important decisions you make on your dissertation journey. This chapter suggested some effective and efficient ways to select a topic and offered seven criteria to consider. Replicating a previous study is often desirable and appropriate since knowledge accumulates through studies that build on each other over time.

With the necessary gear and a topic that interests you, the next step is obtaining expert guides to help you reach the peak. The next chapter concentrates on selecting and working with your dissertation advisor, committee members, and others responsible for guiding the dissertation process.

5

Creating Your
Dissertation Team

Peak Principle: Always Climb Fully Equipped

Climbing high mountains without being fully equipped is folly. Being fully equipped includes having expert guides. Exposure, high winds, treacherous ledges, bone-chilling cold, and unpredictable weather pose grave dangers for the novice climber. To reach the top and return safely, you must have knowledge of where, when, and how to climb. This kind of knowledge comes only from expert guides.

Expert guides are people who have already been where you want to go. They possess the wisdom of experience, know the terrain, and can assess the abilities and limitations of those being guided. Expert guides also inspire confidence and convey what must be done to accomplish the goal. For your survival, you must have absolute confidence and trust in their abilities and be willing to go along with their instructions.

Don't take the journey to EdD or PhD lightly, for there are multiple challenges and obstacles along the way. Selecting a dissertation advisor is the most vital decision you make; that's the person you rely on to help you face the challenges and overcome the obstacles. This person's primary responsibility is to guide your work. He or she becomes your *significant other* throughout the entire dissertation process. Thus, it behooves you to select wisely.

Selecting a Dissertation Advisor

The dissertation advisor's main role is to offer advice and counsel during each phase of the dissertation process. He or she helps you develop and refine your research topic and methodology, critiques multiple drafts of each chapter of the dissertation, and guides you through the proposal and oral defense meetings. In addition, your advisor provides encouragement, shepherds you through any roadblocks, and acknowledges your good work. However, his or her ultimate responsibility lies in ensuring that you produce a high-quality dissertation—one relevant and useful to the field and one that meets your university's standards of scholarly research. Your work reflects not only your own scholarship but also that of your advisor. Your professional reputation and that of your advisor and university are all on the line when someone reads your dissertation.

Criteria for Selecting an Advisor

Ongoing program evaluations conducted at my university found that the top five factors most helpful to students in completing their dissertations dealt with the student-advisor relationship. These five factors, in order of their significance, were the following:

1. Student-chair compatibility

2. Chair reliability

3. Chair responsiveness

4. Chair understanding of student's needs

5. Chair accessibility

These results suggest some criteria you might use in considering your choice of an advisor. Before making that choice, take time to investigate and get to know potential advisors. You might talk with students who worked with a particular advisor, read dissertations chaired by an individual with whom you are interested in working, or take potential advisors to lunch and explore their interest in your topic.

Advisors exhibit a broad array of expertise, style, and personality; plus, they have different expectations of advisees. In selecting a compatible advisor, an important criterion is the level of comfort you feel with that person. Does the person's style of working match your own preferences? For example, do you prefer working with someone directive and highly structured (who closely monitors your work, adheres strictly to timelines, holds regular meetings, etc.), or do you prefer someone more laissez-faire (who waits to be contacted by you, allows more leeway to follow your own leanings, expects a greater amount of independent thinking, etc.)? Do you need nurturing and much support along the way, or are you a confident, independent worker?

Which advising style fits you? Which is most compatible with your needs? As you consider your choice, keep in mind some additional criteria:

1. The person likes your topic. *It is not necessary that the advisor be an expert in your topic.* Compatibility is often more important than expertise. However, it then becomes crucial that at least one committee member possesses expertise in your research area or methodology.

2. The person reads drafts in a timely manner.

3. The person makes sound, helpful comments and suggestions.

4. The person is accessible—willing to talk with you or meet regularly with you.

5. The person is sensitive to your needs yet demands quality work.

The best advisor is one who can be your ally, advocate, and adversary when he or she needs to be.

Selecting the Committee

The dissertation committee usually consists of three or five members (including the advisor), depending on the type of degree and each university's policy. Preferably, these members possess earned doctorates and are highly regarded professionals in their field. Select them for their ability to make specific and useful contributions to your study. These contributions might be expertise in the topic, methodology, or analysis used in the study or the ability to easily access the study's population.

The committee's primary responsibility lies in contributing new ideas, suggestions, and insights for each chapter. In addition, the committee judges the worth and quality of your dissertation and its defense. Committee members should participate actively in all phases of the dissertation process. Early involvement contributes to their sense of ownership in the dissertation and helps eliminate any surprises at the oral defense. They should not be considered "rubber stamps" of the advisor.

Choose the committee in concert with your advisor. Always discuss prospective committee members with your advisor *before* issuing invitations to them to participate in your study.

The same criteria used to select an advisor are appropriate for selecting committee members, but because of their secondary role in the dissertation process, they are less crucial. A compatible advisor and helpful committee members contribute greatly to your success in completing a scholarly dissertation.

The Care and Nurture of Advisors and Committee Members

A good working relationship with your advisor and committee is vital to finishing your dissertation. I offer the following as a guide for obtaining the help and support needed in your journey to become a doctor.

RULE 1

Always Submit Drafts of Your Best Work

Resist the temptation to submit drafts that are not carefully thought out, organized, or well written. It is inappropriate to throw something together in the hope that it gets approved or that your advisor will think and edit for you. With a polished draft, your committee can focus its feedback on substance rather than style and format. Take time to carefully proofread each page. You can pick up many mistakes by reading it aloud to yourself or to another. It also helps to have a critical friend read it over before you submit it to the committee. Very often committee members' initial impressions are lasting ones. David Sternberg (1981) said it well:

> It has been my experience as a dissertation adviser and editor/ consultant for several publishers that the reader's attitudes and appraisal of a manuscript are disproportionately shaped by the first draft which comes to his [or her] attention. If the first impression is unfavorable, successive drafts—even substantially revised ones—never quite erase the memory or smell of the first stinker. (p. 131)

Sloppy, careless work is unappreciated, and it reflects an attitude that you willingly cut corners and don't care about quality. It also shows a lack of respect for your committee's time. Always do your best work with each draft you submit.

RULE 2

Accept Criticism With Grace and Nondefensiveness

Your dissertation should reflect scholarly research and, as such, requires quality thinking and writing that is clear, concise, and cohesive. Expect to make multiple revisions to create such a document. It is critical that you accept your committee's feedback without getting your feelings hurt or being defensive. Develop professional maturity, and remember the committee's job is to provide comments and suggestions that strengthen your study and ensure that it adheres to your university's high standards. Show that you are teachable, flexible, and open to the committee's advice.

RULE 3

Always Incorporate Your Committee's Recommendations for Revisions

Committee members spend considerable time reading and critiquing your drafts. Usually, they are conscientious about making suggestions for improvement. It is not OK to ignore their suggestions. They trust you to incorporate their ideas into your study. Be sure to indicate on your return drafts where you incorporated their suggestions (boldfaced, colored highlighter, or italics, or in a personal note to them). Often, suggestions are negotiable. If you disagree with any of the changes suggested by a committee member, call that person to discuss the situation. Present your ideas persuasively and with tact and diplomacy. Show that you are flexible and open to their opinions rather than defensive of your own position. Such an approach resolves your differences in an amiable fashion.

RULE 4

Respect Your Committee's Time Constraints

Faculty are busy people and must be given sufficient lead time to respond to drafts and inquiries. Don't demand instant turnaround or immediate appointments. However, it is reasonable to ask when a response might be forthcoming. A comment that all advisors dread hearing is, "I realize I've taken six months to revise Chapter 1, but would you be able to read it by tomorrow?" One professor explained,

"Bad planning on your part does not constitute an emergency on mine." Do keep to your timeline as much as possible. Often, faculty members make decisions about adding additional advisees based on when you plan to complete your dissertation.

RULE 5

Keep a Positive, Cheerful Attitude

Enthusiasm engenders enthusiasm and makes working with you so much more pleasant. Your committee wants you to have a positive experience. If you appear morose and whiny, it negatively affects your working relationship. Even if you don't feel positive and cheerful, fake it!

RULE 6

Take the Initiative, but Expect Guidance

An important goal in writing a dissertation is developing the ability to work independently. You need advice and counsel along the way, but it is your responsibility to determine the direction of the research, manage your time, and persist in getting the work done. Take control of your own dissertation. What do you want to know? What is important to you? A good advisor encourages you to make your own decisions; after all, it is *your* dissertation. Don't wait to be told what to do. It delights your advisor when you bring fresh ideas and new insights and perspectives about your study. Keep self-sufficiency and dependence in proper balance. It's up to you to succeed.

RULE 7

Maintain Contact

Schedule regular meetings (at least once a month for one hour) with your advisor to discuss progress and to get advice on specific problems you may be having. It helps keep you in his or her memory, helps to maintain the relationship, and shows your commitment to completing the dissertation in a timely manner.

Consider making regular progress reports to your committee. Mauch and Birch (1993) believed this to be the "single most effective way to stay in touch in a constructive way with each committee member" (p. 134). Their suggested format is as follows:

Project title: _____

From: _____ To: _____

Date: _____

Period covered: _____

Investigator's telephone: _____

Activities completed: _____

Activities continued: _____

Activities initiated: _____

Problems: _____

Other: _____

In addition to sending a written progress report by mail, fax, or e-mail, you should also make a telephone contact every month or six weeks to keep communication channels open.

Be sure to seek advice when you need it. Often, students inhibit themselves in this regard and don't want to appear ignorant or incompetent. It is easy for advisors to overestimate the depth of their students' knowledge. Just don't be a pest! Remember to share the joy of discovery as well as the obstacles overcome.

Adhering to these seven rules creates a more harmonious relationship with your advisor and committee members and ensures a relationship based on mutual respect and shared responsibility.

How to Approach a Potential Advisor

Faculty can choose which dissertations they will or will not chair. Following appropriate etiquette improves your chance of obtaining the advisor you want. First of all, be adequately steeped in the literature related to your topic so you can talk intelligently about it. Also, prepare a well-thought-out prospectus or proposal to show a potential advisor. This document should clearly define the problem and methodology of your study. If done well, it provides insights into the clarity of your thinking and writing—something advisors look for in potential advisees.

Next, give your prospectus or proposal to a potential advisor and request an appointment to discuss it. Be direct about your situation—are you shopping for an advisor or have you decided on one? Don't expect an agreement to chair your dissertation right away, and don't feel rejected if you get a "no." Typically, faculty turn away students if they are overcommitted, not interested in the topic, or do not feel comfortable with the methodology or analysis procedures. Sometimes they are just not willing to work with a particular individual.

What If No One Agrees to Be Your Advisor?

At this point, you need to ask yourself why no one will chair your dissertation and do some soul-searching. Here are some common reasons why potential advisors turn students down:

1. *The topic.* It's too broad and ill defined; it may be trivial, poorly thought out, or they are just not interested in the topic.

2. *Students lack academic skills.* The time and agony of working with poor writers, superficial thinkers, or those known for cutting corners are not worth the effort.

3. *Personal attributes.* Students who are antagonistic, abrasive, stubborn, or undependable always have a hard time convincing a faculty member to chair their dissertation.

You need to appraise your situation and decide where you might need to change. Perhaps you should adjust your behavior and attitude or get some professional help with specific skills you may lack. It is hard to overcome a negative reputation.

At my university, the dean assigns an advisor for you if all faculty members turned you down. This means that the professor assigned has no choice in the matter and must work with you whether or not he or she likes it. This is not a good place to be.

Choosing Outfitters and Bearers (Other Specialized Consultants)

In addition to expert guides, difficult climbs also require outfitters and bearers. You can only reach a high goal with help from other people. Be smart and use all the resources available to you. There are consultants (editors, statisticians, research specialists, etc.) you can call on for expert help and advice. There are campus services available for your use, as well as supportive, caring faculty and student peers eager to help you on your way. Going it alone can be inefficient and costly—it may even cost you your degree. Choose your guides and mentors carefully and then heed their advice and counsel.

Technical Assistance

Often, students require assistance with the technical aspects of writing a dissertation. Getting help with questionnaire design and statistical analysis is reasonable. Unless you were the valedictorian of your statistics class, it behooves you to consult a statistician; however, it is vital that you know enough about statistics to understand his or her advice. An experienced statistician can assist you with analysis techniques, interpretation of the numbers generated, table presentations, and technical writing. He or she should act as a tutor to help you understand why a particular test was used and what the results mean. However, you are responsible for understanding your statistics and defending their use at your oral defense.

Writing Assistance

Consider using an editor throughout the dissertation process. Committee members do some editing; however, their primary role is to assist you with conceptual clarity. They appreciate receiving drafts that pass the literacy test. An editor can be a close friend skilled in grammar who understands dissertation-style writing. If your writing leaves a bit to be desired, then definitely hire a professional. It saves you hours of grief and a multitude of drafts. Just remember that editorial assistance for a dissertation is permissible and encouraged, but *only in matters of style, not content.*

Word Processing Typist

It takes a tremendous amount of skill to prepare tables, figures, and so forth and to type the dissertation manuscript in the appropriate style format. The final document has to be *precisely* in the style required by your university. Most students do not possess this expertise nor do they have time to learn it. Therefore, my advice is *don't do your own final copy.* Type it yourself through the oral defense, if you wish, but then hire a professional to complete the final copy. This saves you much anxiety, time, and money. Be sure to contract with a typist early in the dissertation process. Provide an approximate date when you will hand over your manuscript.

Where to Locate Specialists

Check with your own university to see if there is a list of experts available to assist you. Also, the ASGS website, www.asgs.org has a database of professional consultants (editors, word processors, and writing consultants). The names are arranged according to expertise areas and geographic location. You can click on a name and view detailed information, including services and hourly rates. Another good way to locate reliable technical specialists is to simply ask prior dissertation students and university faculty whom they know and recommend. Try to get at least two names so you can have a choice and not feel tied to someone with whom you may not be compatible.

Once you have a list of names, contact them. Let them know who recommended them and share your timetable for completing the dissertation. Also, let them know what kind of help you need and find out if they have the time to assist you and what they charge.

Summary

Selecting an advisor and committee members is one of the most vital decisions you make. Ideally, these individuals should like your topic, make helpful suggestions, return drafts in a timely manner, be accessible, and hold you accountable for quality work. In this chapter, I suggested seven rules to help you maintain a good working relationship with your advisor and committee members and offered guidance in observing appropriate etiquette when approaching a potential advisor. Other available resources to help you complete the dissertation are statisticians, editors, typists, and so on.

Your preparation for the climb thus far included filling your backpack with the inner essentials, identifying a topic to research, and selecting expert guides, outfitters, and bearers. The next chapter centers on peer dissertation support groups and provides strategies on their formation and structure.

6

Dissertation Support Groups

The fact that only about 40% to 50% of doctoral students complete their degrees is a consistent research finding. Even though the reasons vary considerably, the issue of support—kind and amount—usually affects this attrition in some way. Sources of support come from family, other students, consultants, and faculty. You enhance your chance of obtaining your doctorate when you deliberately seek out all sources of support.

Chapter 5 described the role of advisors, committee members, and other consultants and how they support you along the journey. This chapter focuses on peer dissertation support groups and offers general guidelines on their formation, goals, and organization.

Joining a support group provides both emotional and academic support during the dissertation process. Researching and writing a dissertation can be lonely and isolating. For the most part, it is a solitary journey. It's easy to drop out when you feel as if no one understands or cares. So surrounding yourself with people who empathize and support you can be a valuable asset.

Few people outside your doctoral peer group understand what you're going through emotionally or have a clue about how to help you academically. Support-group members understand your dilemmas and frustrations and help lift your spirits. They provide an ear to listen, a shoulder to cry on, and a foot to boost you back on track when necessary. They help you when you're stuck. They are your cheering squad and reliable critics who contribute valuable insight and suggestions from conceptualizing a research topic to improving your written drafts.

Critical Decisions

There are no clear-cut rules for creating a viable dissertation support group. Each group must determine its own goals, expectations, and working procedures. But before jumping into a group or attempting to create one, some critical decisions should be made if the group is to survive and benefit all members. Here are some to consider:

- Should the group have a formal leader, rotate leadership, or be leaderless?
- What are the group's goals? What does each person want from the group? (Primarily academic—focused on critiquing written drafts or discussing methodology? Primarily support—focused on providing social and emotional support for personal problems?)
- How many members should there be? Need they be at the same stage in the dissertation process?
- How often and for how long should the group meet? Where?
- What norms should be established? What will happen if someone consistently violates the norms (chronically late, fail to bring a promised draft, etc.)?

Strategies and Structures of Successful Support Groups

What strategies and structures have effective dissertation support groups used? In the 1992 *Dissertation News* (Vol. 8), 12 rules for forming and structuring support groups were suggested. Additional suggestions were added in 1997 in the Association for Support of Graduate Students (ASGS) "Best of Doc Talk." (See www.asgs.org; reprinted with permission from ASGS.)

They are as follows:

1. Get at least 5 students (some will drop; less than 4 doesn't allow enough diversity) with different backgrounds in your field (a methodologist, a good writer, a computer whiz, etc.). Members should be of about the same academic caliber so they all feel they're getting as much as they're giving.

2. Meet once a week and give all members a copy of everybody's dissertation at the first session. It may be that some groups might best meet infrequently—say once a month—to accommodate members' jobs and family obligations.

3. Feature 2 members' research per meeting, about 45 minutes each.

4. Provide each member an abstract of what will be discussed, at least 3 days before meetings.

5. Keep criticism constructive, with suggestions for improvement. A key to your support group's success is for everyone to know how to make supportive criticisms.

6. Agree to spend 3 hours each week (1 to read and critique; 2 to meet). Be clear about what activities you'll expect group members to carry out and how much time you expect members to devote to the group. Will students read each other's chapter drafts and make comments? What kind of comments (conceptual, organizational, editorial, etc.) will they be expected to make?

7. Have each member tape record the session focusing on his or her dissertation.

8. End each meeting with 15 minutes for members to report progress and mention specific problems.

9. Restrict discussions to dissertation matters only.

10. If you have less than 4 students, postpone the meeting. Otherwise, presenting students won't get a variety of viewpoints.

11. Get written agreement for confidentiality at the first session, so everyone can speak openly, even about faculty or other students.

12. Acknowledge dissertation victories. Celebrate accomplishments such as getting the dissertation approved and passing the defense.

Other successful strategies students use at my university are *contingency enforcement* and *timeline monitoring*. Contingency enforcement means that when a group member fails to accomplish a stated dissertation goal or task or meet a specific deadline, or misses a meeting, the group enforces that person's contingency plan. The plan might be as simple as buying lottery tickets for all, paying for everyone's meal, or even sending a check to an organization despised by the "errant" student. They are also good at laying on guilt trips and threatening public disgrace—all in good fun!

These support groups bond students in significant and touching ways. They frequently attend each other's oral defense and take notes so their friend can concentrate on the feedback he or she receives. Group members often become lifetime friends who creatively celebrate each other's successes even beyond the dissertation years. They have great times together, laughing and sharing the joys and sorrows of dissertating. Some groups stay together until the last person graduates, having faithfully attended each other's graduation ceremony and party.

Students also help each other monitor dissertation timelines. Each student brings to the support group meeting his or her projected timeline for completing the dissertation. The timeline consists of all major tasks to be completed, from obtaining an advisor to making final revisions. They are held accountable by the group for staying on that timeline.

⚠ CAVEAT

Select group members carefully. There are certain personality types that make group work difficult and tiresome. Domineering types; shy, retiring types; and negative thinkers place considerable stress on a group. Also, there are those who are extremely needy emotionally and drain the group's energy by asking everyone to help them cope. For the group to be satisfying, all participants need to both give and take equally—to critique and be critiqued.

Other Considerations

Rather than joining a support group, consider working with one other person—a dissertation buddy. Someone you know well and with whom you are very compatible could be more efficient than a larger group. In today's world, you might consider creating a virtual support group. With compatible software and computer skills, it seems the same amount of support could be given online through chat rooms, online editorial critiques, online coaches (faculty or competent alumni), and so on.

Summary

Consider joining a peer dissertation support group. It can provide both emotional and academic support during the dissertation process. However, before creating or joining a dissertation support group, consider the following: type of leadership, individual needs, numbers of members, stage in the dissertation process, and time schedules. This chapter identified some successful strategies that could enhance the support group's effectiveness. In lieu of a dissertation support group, consider working with a dissertation buddy or creating a virtual support group.

Before beginning the climb up the mountain, you should pay attention to organizing yourself. The next chapter provides helpful hints on organizing your workspace and your time, working smart, and maintaining balance in your life.

7

Organizing Yourself

Organizing is what you do before you do something so that when you do it, it's not all mixed up.

—Christopher Robin in
A. A. Milne's *Winnie the Pooh*

Successfully completing your dissertation requires organization and planning. Working hard is not enough, you must also work smart. Working smart means organizing a place conducive to writing and developing a time schedule to which you faithfully adhere even if you lack inspiration. Knowing yourself, the peaks and ebbs of your energy patterns, is also essential to efficiently getting the job done. Working smart also requires maintaining balance in your life. Today, many doctoral students are married with children and hold full-time jobs, making it essential to balance dissertation activities and other life obligations. This chapter offers suggestions for organizing your workspace, your time, and yourself for effective dissertating and for maintaining balance in the process. Think of these suggestions as options. Try them out to see which ones work for you.

Organize Your Workspace

It is extremely important that you find a suitable place for dissertating where you can be productive. Determine where you do your best work, and plan to be there each time you work on the dissertation. Your dissertation workspace may be your office at work, your office at home, or a separate area in your home designed exclusively for your dissertation work. It should be quiet, private, and free of interruptions and distractions such as posters, TV, fish tank, portraits, and pleasure books. Let the answering machine take phone messages while you work. If music helps you write, then keep CDs or your iPod handy. Relegate to this office only those activities related to the dissertation—no writing letters, paying bills, or surfing the Internet. Having a single-minded focus makes you much more efficient. Wherever you work, make sure you have the following:

- Computer and printer
- Comfortable, ergonomic chair
- Sturdy, decent-sized desk
- Good lighting
- Appropriate reference materials (dictionary, thesaurus, style manual, etc.)
- Necessary materials (printer ink cartridges, etc.)
- Bookcase
- Filing cabinet
- File folders
- Writing materials (pens, pencils, sticky notes, tablets, etc.)
- "Ideas" notebook to jot down ideas that come to you

An organized workspace dedicated exclusively to your dissertation study goes a long way toward maintaining optimum efficiency.

Organize Your Time

Because no deadlines are imposed on you while writing the dissertation, time can escape quite easily. Completing a dissertation requires that you manage your time well. Realistically assess how much time you can devote to your dissertation study. It is a big challenge to *find time* in an already busy daily schedule. The reality is that you have to *make time*. Those who don't, relegate themselves to the title ABD (all-but-dissertation).

Planning and scheduling time are the keys to making things happen. Planning is deciding *what* to do. Scheduling is deciding *when* to do it—picking the time to do the activities. It is more like a commitment, whereas planning is the intention. *Scheduled things tend to happen.* To be truly efficient, create at least three scheduling plans. First, design an overall dissertation timeline, which helps you see the big picture and keeps you on track. Second, create a time schedule to which you commit so many hours each day or week. Third, create a to-do list—a daily reminder of the tasks that need to be done each day. The following describes these three techniques and offers some recommendations to make them work for you.

1. The Dissertation Timeline

The Gantt chart—a useful method for creating a dissertation timeline—can be as detailed as you wish. To construct a Gantt chart, list the major phases or specific activities of the dissertation down the left side of the page. Across the top, list the time for completing the entire dissertation process. Then, create a bar graph that shows the beginning and ending times for each major phase or activity. When creating this long-range plan, it helps to work backwards from commencement. When do you need to turn in the dissertation to your graduate office? To do that, when would you need to defend? To do that, when would you need to get it to the committee? See Appendix A for an example of a Gantt chart.

2. Time Schedule

Creating a *strict* schedule of hours each day or week to work on your dissertation is essential. I cannot emphasize this enough. No real progress can be made without ongoing involvement with your study. Otherwise, you spin your wheels trying to figure out where you left off the last time. Try to schedule as many unbroken hours as possible for uninterrupted concentration. I find that in a block of two hours, I can make considerable progress. As much as possible, maintain daily progress—even if it is only 15 minutes at a time. This way your mind stays focused and your subconscious working. It helps to set a goal for how much work you will accomplish each day or week and to keep a record to determine if your goal was met. This keeps you moving and motivated.

> **REMEMBER**
>
> - Plan each day. Block out 30 minutes, an hour, three hours, or whatever time you can to work on your dissertation.
> - Choose a scheduling strategy that works for you. You may choose to work in terms of hours and minutes worked or pages written. Figure out which works best for you.
> - Stick to your schedule.

3. To-Do List

In the time management literature, experts suggest myriad techniques for managing a To-Do list. Some recommend listing everything that needs to be done and reviewing the list first thing in the morning to confront items that still need to be done. Others recommend keeping a short, doable To-Do list. They say you should place only three to six items on your To-Do list and make sure you accomplish them. This forces the habit of finishing what you place on your list and results in a feeling of accomplishment.

One good way to be efficient is to write out a To-Do list every day. Separate your To-Do list into A, B, and C priorities. *A* items are your high-priority activities; *B* items may be urgent but not as important; *C* items are those that would be nice to do if you get the time. Start with the A items—the ones that must be done. Then move to the B items—the ones that probably should be done. C items are least important. Don't work on a C just because it's easy to do. Check off items as you complete them to give yourself a sense of accomplishment.

Another way to prioritize your To-Do list is found in the book *Time Tactics of Very Successful People* by Griessman (1994). He suggested you prioritize by asking the following questions of each item:

- Will it help me do my thesis or otherwise make my life better?
- Does it have a real deadline that will cost me if I miss it?
- Is it a command from someone I can't ignore?
- Will it help me fulfill my potential?
- Will it matter a year from now?

It makes little difference which type of priority technique you use as long as it works for you. The main thing is to develop the habit of first things first.

💡 HELPFUL HINT

Be sure to keep your To-Do list handy, on your bulletin board or day planner or in your purse or pocket.

Working Smart

Working hard is not enough—you need to work smart to ensure that the hours you schedule for dissertation work are truly productive ones. Developing efficient habits and routines and applying the various techniques described in this book are some of the ways you can work with the least amount of wasted time, motion, and money. Here are some recommendations for working smart.

1. Work on Your Dissertation
During Times That You Are Most Productive

Are you a night owl?

or

Are you an early bird?

Pay attention to your biorhythms. Determine the hours most productive for you and try to schedule those hours for dissertation work—your number one priority. If you're an early bird, consider rising two hours earlier than usual; if a night owl, stay up two hours later. Schedule routine tasks for your low-energy periods and your dissertation tasks when you're alert and energetic. It's more productive to work with your daily rhythms and ride your energy peaks.

2. Learn to Say No

Learn to say no to nonvital, trivial requests. In the book *Secrets for a Successful Dissertation* (Fitzpatrick, Secrist, & Wright, 1998), the authors expressed this idea well:

Are you able to say no to favors, fun times, fund-raising, chair positions, family reunions, and frolicking in the park on Sunday afternoons? Because if you are ever going to gain control over your days and nights, and manage your time efficiently, the first lesson to learn is to say no. Say it regretfully, say it remorsefully, say it with clenched teeth, or say it with joy—but say it loud and clear. The world is Full of Time Zappers who will steal your time if you allow them, so put all your good deeds on hold and use the word *no* freely. You'll be glad you did. (p. 97)

Practice making responses such as, "I'm sorry, I'm not available that night," "I can't do that task today, but how about next week?" "How about asking John instead?" or "What would you like me to give up to do this?" *Be gracious with people, but be firm with time.*

> Life can get away from us through thousands of little dribs and drabs.
>
> —B. E. Griessman

Your dissertation year is not the time to be president or chairperson of anything, take on additional responsibilities, give a presentation, or attend a conference. Eliminate unnecessary activities and accept only those obligations you consider absolutely necessary. You must be ruthless with your time and energy. Learn to say no when you should, and learn to say it *without guilt*.

3. Schedule Frequent "Joy Breaks"

Throughout your working time, stop and do something pleasurable. Stretch, move about, take some deep breaths, play with your dog, make some tea, or take a walk. These activities energize you and keep you focused. Also, the mind is quite remarkable. When allowed to wander, it often comes up with creative ideas and decisions. You must let your body and mind rest to do your best creative work.

4. Know Your Timewasters

Two useful tasks to maintain maximum efficiency are (a) determine those things that waste your time and (b) work on reducing or eliminating them. Develop a mind-set that judges every activity in terms of whether it brings you closer to completing your dissertation. People must learn to respect your time as much as you do. Make a list of 5 to 10 timewasters in your life and then prioritize in order of importance. Determine what you think might be the cause(s) of each timewaster and generate some possible solutions to reduce or eliminate each one.

5. Reward Your Efforts

Behavior persists when it is rewarded, so give yourself rewards along the way. When you meet a deadline, have coffee with a friend, do a crossword puzzle, rent a movie, buy yourself an ice cream, or do something else that makes you feel good about your accomplishment. Tell yourself you can't do that thing until you accomplish the allotted amount of dissertation work. Punishments can also work. Some people find it useful to say, "If I don't get this done by that date, then I can't do _____."

Maintain Balance

Finding the right balance between your dissertation and the rest of your life is difficult. All work and no play puts considerable pressure on you. It causes illness, depression, burnout, and exhaustion. Most doctoral students I have known report the first thing that goes is their fitness routine. They also mention the strain the dissertation causes in family relationships.

Having a life beyond the dissertation is important. To finish, you need to put the dissertation first. This means putting other life areas on hold from time to time. However, you needn't always give up other important life activities and devote every waking moment to your dissertation. Working all the time will likely lead to burnout.

One way to get a handle on balancing your life while dissertating is to write down all the things most important in your life (health, family, friends, hobbies, fun, etc.). Then you can identify strategies to help keep them in balance.

Strategies for Getting a Life While Dissertating

1. Take Care of Your Body

Because you must be well to do your best work, remember to get plenty of rest and eat nutritious meals. Also, there is considerable evidence about the benefits of deep breathing and regular exercise to your well-being. The extra oxygen sent to the brain provides energy and helps you think more clearly and creatively. It is also considered a stress buster.

2. Increase Family Support

To maintain family support, block out hours during the week for family and friends. For example, agree that Saturday nights are available for socializing with friends, Wednesday and Friday nights plus Sunday are reserved for family time. Such a plan maintains positive and healthy relationships with the important people in your life. In addition, it cuts down on the guilt so many students feel when these vital relationships are ignored. If you stay true to these time commitments, your friends and family can readily adjust to the schedule.

Another recommendation is to keep your family and friends informed about how you're progressing on the dissertation and even involve them as much as possible. Children love being a part of something so significant in your life. Let them experience your university campus firsthand, and include them in all celebratory activities.

> The key to completing a dissertation is not brilliance or even inspiration, but organization.
>
> —David Sternberg (1981)

Organizing effectively is critical to your success in the dissertation journey. It takes time to learn to be efficient with your time, but it's well worth the effort. I do hope you try some of these techniques.

Summary

Make organization and planning a top priority in your dissertation journey. It is important to organize your workspace so you can concentrate and be productive. It is equally important to organize your time to maximize energy and keep on track. Create at least three scheduling plans: (a) an overall dissertation timeline, (b) a daily or weekly schedule, and (c) a To-Do list. Work smart by developing efficient habits and routines such as (a) working at a time when you are most productive, (b) learning to say no, (c) scheduling frequent joy breaks, (d) knowing your timewasters, and (e) rewarding your efforts. Maintain balance between your dissertation and the rest of your life by taking care of your body and increasing family support.

Following the guidelines and recommendations presented thus far puts you firmly on the path and ready to begin the climb to the top. The next chapter helps you acquire the skills of using the Internet and technology to conduct research throughout the various phases of writing a dissertation and offers tips to keep you sane and productive in the process.

PART III

Beginning the Climb

The journey of a thousand miles begins and ends with one step.

—Lao Tse

8

Using the Internet and Technology to Conduct Research

Become computer literate and Internet savvy! You don't need to become a computer geek, but you do need to understand how to exploit your computer to make your dissertation research easier. It behooves you to become a power user of your computer and its major programs. There certainly are downsides to computers. Any user knows the frustration of crashes, lost files, and inoperable software. But for the most part, it will be your best friend and most essential tool for completing your dissertation. Hardware and software advances continue to make conducting research more and more efficient.

Technology and the Internet may be used in a variety of ways throughout the dissertation process. They may be used for the following.

Numerous software packages are available to help you in each of the areas listed. It is beyond the scope of this book to provide in-depth information. Several online resources, books, and articles are available to assist you. I will, however, offer some resources and helpful tips for using the Internet and technology in the research process.

Writing the Dissertation

- Word processing
- Editing and revising
- Spelling
- Thesaurus
- Outlining and mind mapping
- Style
- Other writing aids—Internet
- Speech recognition software

Preparing Surveys

- Mailing labels
- Survey processor
- Desktop publishing

Collecting and Analyzing Data

- Fax
- E-mail
- Interview notes (software for voice input)
- Database for tracking
- Statistical analysis
- Qualitative analysis
- Questionnaires on e-mail and websites
- Computerized polling
- Digital tablets

Conducting Literature Searches

- Online access to libraries
- Internet search engines
- Online databases
- CD-ROM searches
- Online note cards
- Abstracts
- Scanning
- Managing bibliographies

Communicating Via the Internet

- E-mail
- Wikis
- Discussion groups and forums
- World Wide Web indexes and data
- Chat rooms
- UseNet news groups
- Weblogs (blogs)
- Conferencing software

Conducting Literature Searches

⚠ CAVEAT

Remember, anyone can put whatever they like on the Web. The information may or may not be accurate. Always be a critical and careful consumer of information and ensure that the information source is valid. Refereed journals, books, and so on are still the key to high-quality information collection.

To conduct an effective literature search requires specific knowledge and skills. You should become familiar with search engines and how they work (e.g., using key words, Boolean operators, truncation, and online help).

Search Engines

Search engines are tools designed to scan the World Wide Web for sites and pages, which are then stored in indexes or databases. You search the contents of databases by typing selected keywords in the text box located on the search engine's home page. The search engine then retrieves documents that match your keywords and displays the results ranked in order of that engine's relevance.

Comparisons of Search Engines

The three major search engines used today are Google (www.google .com), Yahoo! Search (http://search.yahoo.com), and Ask.com (www .ask.com). A search engine for scholarly or academic links is Google Scholar (http://scholar.google.com). You will find many peer-reviewed articles, books, and so on, as well as how often they are cited in other publications.

A table detailing the features of recommended search engines was developed by the Teaching Library at the University of California at Berkeley (www.lib.berkeley.edu/TeachingLib/Guides/Internet/Search Engines.html).

There are also specialty search engines and virtual libraries in different disciplines, such as the WWW Virtual Library for Anthropology (www.anthropologie.net) or for Sociology (http://socserv.mcmaster .ca/w3virtsoclib), and so on.

You can find listings for a variety of specialty search engines at SearchEngineGuide (www.searchengineguide.com/searchengines.html).

A valuable resource for searching the "Deep Web" (a vast repository of information not accessible by search engines and directories) may be found on the Online College Blog titled "Useful Tips and Tools to Research the Deep Web." The author provides tips, strategies, and helpful articles and resources for deep searching (www.online-college-blog .com/index.php/features/100-useful-tips-and-tools-to-research-the-deep-web).

Online Help

Instructions for using search engines are built into the system. Look for online help buttons or links such as "advanced search" and "search tips." Consult online help to learn the following:

- How to enter searches
- What truncation symbol to use
- How to display results
- How to print or download records

Evaluating Websites

Since anyone can post information on the Internet without any oversight or editing or fact checking, it is important that you evaluate any information that you find on the Internet to determine its credibility and authority before using it in your research. Look at the URL to see if it is a personal website, an educational site, a commercial site, or a nonprofit organization site. Look for authorship of the site (is there an "About Us" link somewhere on the page?) and when the page was last updated. Does the site try to persuade or to sell something, or is it simply providing information? Is there any bias that you can detect? Can you validate the information through another source? The Teaching Library at the University of California at Berkeley has another excellent guide on evaluating web pages (www.lib.berkeley.edu/TeachingLib/Guides/ Internet/Evaluate.html).

Social Networking on the Web (Web 2.0)

Social media is becoming an important tool for research. The emerging power of the World Wide Web involves the power of people around the world to post, discuss, and comment on information relevant to them. As a researcher, this power allows you to tap into the knowledge of researchers around the world. According to Ó Dochartaigh (2007), "Web 2.0 is used as a shorthand to describe a new generation of online services that, among other things, integrate writer and reader, producer and consumer and blur the boundaries between both" (p. 99). Some academic journals now promote online discussion and commentary on their published articles. Here are some relevant resources for you to investigate to see how you might be able to use them for your dissertation research.

Blogs

One genre for Web communication is the blog. The term *blog*, a contraction of *web log*, is used for a website with free searchable journals of opinions and links updated daily by an individual or a group displayed in reverse chronological order. They provide commentary on a particular subject, describe events, or function as personal online diaries. Blogs usually combine text, images, and links to other blogs and Web pages related to its topic. An appealing feature of blogs is the ability for readers to leave comments on the items posted. Accessing blogs as a researcher can provide a perspective on your topic that is unavailable elsewhere. According to Ó Dochartaigh (2007), "If your research involves an issue of contemporary controversy, this provides a genuinely novel kind of resource for detailed investigation of the minute details of very specific issues" (p. 100).

Searching Blogs

There are a variety of blog search engines available; however, I found Google Blog Search to be one of the fastest and one that returns posts right on topic. The main focus of Google Blog Search is on relevance, but posts can also be sorted by date (click on the top right of the results page). In addition, you can keep track of new postings in your areas of interest via RSS feeds—short summaries sent from your favorite websites.

Wikis

For group projects, a wiki is a wonderful resource. A wiki is a website that users can change using a web browser. One of the best known wikis is Wikipedia, the encyclopedia created and edited by its users. Since anyone can post to some wikis, you need to be careful to evaluate the information and the credibility of the people posting the information. Do a Google search on a topic such as "bilingual education wikis," and you will find a variety of resources.

Other Helpful Technology

To help in your literature review, consider some technology currently on the market. For example, to personally track your reading, scanners can be very helpful. Three types of scanners are available for scanning text into your computer: a flatbed scanner, a small portable scanner, and a pen scanner. Pen scanners slide over text much like a highlighter and can hold up to 1,000 pages of scanned text. When you're done scanning, you can transfer the text directly to your computer. Think of all the time you can save by bringing your laptop computer and pen scanner to the library when you do your literature search!

The digital tablet is another technology item to consider. You can make hand-written notes directly onto the screen as you would with pen and paper. It is especially useful for drawing graphics that might be difficult to do with a mouse. Your notes and graphics can then transfer to your computer.

The market on personal digital assistants (PDAs) is expanding dramatically. These portable devices keep track of your calendar, contacts, and e-mail. They also exchange information with PCs and other PDAs, download music, allow you to surf the web, and more. Several types are available, such as Windows Powered Pocket PC and Palm OS. One way to find out about these devices is to conduct an Internet search. For example, enter "personal digital assistants" on Google.

Another helpful tool in writing your dissertation is speech recognition software. This software enables a computer to respond to the human voice in place of a keyboard or mouse. You talk, it types! Some products for your consideration are Dragon Naturally Speaking 9 Preferred, Windows Speech Recognition (included with the Windows Vista operating system), and for Macs, MacSpeech Dictate.

You may also obtain a small digital recorder that allows you to input data from anywhere. You can capture meetings, interviews, phone calls, personal thoughts, and so on, which can then be transferred directly into your computer through the speech recognition program. There are several products on the market: Sony, Olympus, and Dragon are some you might look into.

Dissertation support groups might find conferencing software an excellent way to hold web meetings or online conferences. You can find out about two good programs at the following sites: Genesys (www.genesys.com) and Saba Centra (https://na1.saba.com/Default .aspx).

Using the Internet for Data Collection

The Internet has become more than a place to locate and disseminate information; it can be a method of data collection as well. Because of the proliferation of survey authoring software packages and online survey services, collecting data from the Internet has become easier and faster. The following books can assist you with information about survey design and using the Internet to collect survey data.

Best, S., & Krueger, B. (2004). *Internet data collection (quantitative applications in the Social Sciences)*. Thousand Oaks, CA: Sage.

Couper, M. (2008). *Designing effective web surveys*. New York: Cambridge University Press.

Dillman, D. (2007). *Mail and Internet surveys: The tailored design method* (2nd ed.). New York: Wiley.

Sue, V. (2007). *Conducting online surveys*. Thousand Oaks, CA: Sage.

If you are considering conducting a web survey, I highly recommend that you read the following article:

Wright, K. B. (2005). Researching inter-based populations: Advantages and disadvantages of online survey research, online questionnaire authoring software packages, and web survey services. *Journal of Computer-Mediated Communication, 10*(3), article 11. Available from http://jcmc.indiana.edu/ vol10/issue3/wright.html

This very helpful article discusses the advantages and disadvantages of conducting online survey research and evaluates various web survey software packages and online survey-related services in terms of their available features, costs, and limitations.

Another excellent resource that discusses methods of online data access, analysis, and collection is

Rudestam, K. E., & Newton, R. R. (2007). *Surviving your dissertation: A comprehensive guide to content and process.* Thousand Oaks, CA: Sage.

In the chapter titled "Online Data Access and Collection," the authors describe strategies for accessing primary and secondary data and Internet-based data analysis. Included in the chapter are two comprehensive tables that provide (1) data archives and libraries with the name of the site, URL, and comments; and (2) online services for survey design and data collection.

Using Your Library's Electronic Search Capability

It is essential that you become familiar with your university's library. Cultivate a librarian or two who can assist you in learning the ins and outs of the library. Also, most librarians are highly skilled in researching topics, which comes in handy when conducting literature reviews. Many university libraries maintain large collections of electronic databases and online catalogs. Often, you may download full dissertations and theses.

Using Your Instructional Technology Center

Frequently, universities' instructional technology centers provide services for students in the use of technology and multimedia. You may receive technical support and training in various software programs.

Additional Online Resources

Dissertation Doctor	www.dissertationdoctor.com
ASGS	www.asgs.org
Writing and Presenting Your Thesis or Dissertation (S. Joseph Levine, PhD)	www.learnerassociates.net/dissthes
Citation Styles Online (MLA/APA/Chicago/CBE)	www.bedfordstmartins.com/online/citex.html

Tips to Keep You Sane and Productive

As you use your computer to write your dissertation, these tips will prove invaluable.

    1. Become familiar with your computer software and accessories *before* beginning your dissertation research. Familiarity with

technology resources saves you much time and frustration and improves the appearance of your dissertation.

2. Use your required style manual at the outset. It's much easier and saves considerable time if you develop the habit of citing information in the correct style rather than revising it later.

3. Computers crash at very inopportune times, so be sure to *back up all your files regularly* on thumb drives, external hard drives, CDs, or DVDs. Be sure to place them in a place safe from fire, flood, theft, or other catastrophes. You might keep one at the office, at a friend's house, or in a safe-deposit box. Your work is too valuable to lose. Remember that Murphy's Law also prevails in the research world.

4. Save your work as you go along. After every few sentences, click on "Save." You won't regret it. Word processing programs such as Word have a "Save AutoRecover" function. The user can define the frequency down to every one minute. Go to "Word Options," "Save," then click in the "Save AutoRecover info every: ___ minutes" box and change the time to one minute.

5. Buy a surge protector to plug your computer into in case of electricity blackouts or surges. A better protective device is an uninterruptible power supply (UPS). This device allows your computer to keep running for a short time when power is lost. It contains a battery that kicks in when it senses a loss of power, which gives you time to save any data you are working on. When power surges occur, a UPS intercepts the surge so it doesn't damage your computer.

6. Before making revisions, copy your draft into another file with a different name and date it. This way you can keep your original drafts intact. You may decide later that an earlier version was best.

7. Do not borrow software. First of all, it is illegal, and viruses can appear and cause great havoc.

8. Purchase a high-quality virus protection program. Virus protection software such as Symantec's "Norton AntiVirus" and McAfee are designed to prevent or block viruses, worms, Trojan horses, and so on.

REMEMBER

"If anything can go wrong, it will!" And, "If there is a possibility of several things going wrong, the one that will cause the most damage will be the one to go wrong."

Corollary: "If there is a worst time for something to go wrong, it will happen then."

9. Purchase firewall software if you have a DSL- or cable-connected system. It protects you from hackers. The following are three excellent options:

Symantec	www.symantec.com
BlackICE Defender	www.black-ice-firewall.com
ZoneAlarm	www.zonealarm.com

These can be downloaded from the Web. Symantec offers free downloads. BlackICE Defender can be downloaded for purchase. ZoneAlarm has several options available for download and purchase. Firewalls can create access problems with proxy servers, so beware!

10. Pay attention to your physical self while sitting at the computer. Set your computer up ergonomically and use a proper ergonomic chair and good posture. To learn how to set up your workspace for good ergonomics, refer to Pascarelli's (2004) *Dr. Pascarelli's Complete Guide to Repetitive Strain Injury: What You Need to Know About RSI and Carpal Tunnel Syndrome*.

11. Also, consider purchasing a glare protector for your screen to help with eyestrain. There are also special eyeglasses for use while reading a computer screen.

12. Take frequent breaks. Stretch, go for a walk, play with your dog.

Technology continues to change at an amazing pace, which makes it difficult to make too many hard-and-fast recommendations. By the time you read this chapter, it could be obsolete! I attempted to provide the most up-to-date web addresses available; however, because websites constantly change, it is impossible to stay current for any length of time. If you find an invalid website, either because it doesn't exist any longer or the address changed, simply do a key word search on the subject. For the time being, the information contained in this chapter should be helpful as you work with these most important tools—technology and the Internet.

Summary

Learning to use the Internet and technology efficiently saves considerable time in conducting your research. They are valuable tools in all phases of the dissertation process: writing the document, conducting the literature search, preparing surveys, collecting and analyzing data, and communicating via the Internet.

Following the guidelines and recommendations presented thus far puts you firmly on the path and ready to climb to the top. The next chapter helps you acquire the skills to conduct a substantive, comprehensive, and systematic literature review in your field of interest.

9

Reviewing
the Literature

The greatest gift you can give yourself as a researcher is to read and analyze the literature surrounding your study as early as possible. Too often, students see the literature review as something to do while waiting for their data to be collected. This may be because they don't fully understand the importance and purpose of the review. It may also be because they are uncertain of the exact procedures to follow for conducting a literature search. The importance of a literature search is stated by Hart (1998) in his book *Doing a Literature Review:*

> A review of the literature is important because without it you will not acquire an understanding of your topic, of what has already been done on it, how it has been researched, and what the key issues are. In your written project you will be expected to show that you understand previous research on your topic. This amounts to showing that you have understood the main theories in the subject area and how they have been applied and developed, as well as the main criticisms that have been made of work on the topic. (p. 1)

A similar notion was advanced by Boote and Beile (2005) in their article titled, "Scholars Before Researchers: On the Centrality of the Dissertation Literature Review in Research Preparation." They made the following points: "A substantive, thorough, sophisticated literature review is a precondition for doing substantive, thorough, sophisticated research . . . . A researcher cannot perform significant research without first understanding the literature in the field. Not understanding the prior research clearly puts a researcher at a disadvantage" (p. 3).

A comprehensive, up-to-date literature review allows you to get to the frontier in your area of research and, at the same time, become an expert in your field. In addition, the insights and knowledge you gain provide the basis for a better-designed study and enhance the possibility of obtaining significant results. A review of the literature is a vital part of the research process.

A literature review is a two-phase activity. In the first phase you conduct the review by identifying appropriate resources, searching for relevant materials, and analyzing, synthesizing, and organizing the results; the second phase is the actual writing of the review—that which culminates in the completed product. The literature review section of a study is found where reference is made to the related research and theory around your topic. The location may vary depending on your selected methodology. For example, in some qualitative studies, authors might choose to locate the literature section toward the end of the dissertation, following discussion of the emerging theory, which, according to Creswell (2008), "allows the views of the participants to emerge without being constrained by the views of others from the literature" (p. 90). Researchers in quantitative studies typically place their discussion of the literature at the beginning of a study, usually in a separate chapter titled "Review of the Literature." Frequently, the literature is referred to again at the end of the study when comparing the study's findings to the literature.

This chapter helps you acquire the skills to conduct and write a thorough and systematic review of the literature in your field of interest. The chapter includes the purpose and scope of the literature review, notes on its preparation, specific steps in conducting a literature review, and strategies and techniques for writing the literature review.

Purpose and Scope

What is a literature review? According to Creswell (2008), "A literature review is a written summary of journal articles, books, and other documents that describe the past and current state of information; organizes the literature into topics; and documents a need for a proposed study." (p. 89). Reviewing the literature involves locating, analyzing, synthesizing, and organizing previous research and documents (periodicals, books, abstracts, etc.) related to your study area. The goal is to obtain a detailed, cutting-edge knowledge of your particular topic. To do this, you must immerse yourself in your subject by reading extensively and voraciously. A solid and comprehensive review of the literature accomplishes several important purposes. It helps you to do the following:

1. Focus the purpose of your study more precisely

2. Develop a conceptual or theoretical framework that might be used to guide your research

3. Identify key variables for study and suggest relationships among them if you are completing a quantitative study; if you are conducting a qualitative study, identify the concepts or topics you plan to study

4. Provide a historical background for your study

5. Uncover previous research similar to your own that can be meaningfully extended

6. Determine the relationship of your topic relative to current and past studies

7. Identify scholars and theorists in your area of study

8. Form a basis for determining the significance of your study

9. Uncover questionnaires or tests previously validated

10. Link your findings to previous studies (Do your findings support or contradict them?)

I hope I convinced you of the importance of doing an early and comprehensive review of the literature. The benefits are numerous, especially in the initial stages of designing a dissertation study.

One of the biggest frustrations students encounter is determining how long and how comprehensive the review should be. Even though you must read broadly to develop perspective about your topic, don't make the mistake of thinking that you must include in the bibliography every book, article, or study read. The literature review is not an aggregation of every book and article related to your topic; it is always selective. Therefore, you must be discriminating and include only the most relevant information. Remember that *bigger is not better!* The shotgun approach indicates a lack of knowledge about what is relevant information. Unfortunately, no magic formula exists to guide your selection; it is a judgment call on your part. You know it is time to quit when you keep encountering the same references and can't find important new resources.

Generally speaking, most advisors prefer the literature review chapter to be around 20 to 40 pages. However, keep in mind that this can vary depending on the breadth and complexity of your study and the preferences of your advisor. Take time to clarify with your advisor his or her preferences prior to writing the review.

Preparation

In much the same way your advisor becomes your significant other during the dissertation process, the library becomes your second home. Much time is spent there, and it behooves you to completely familiarize yourself with the library before starting your literature review. Know what references are available and where to find them, what services the library provides, and the regulations and procedures regarding the use of library materials. Spend time browsing the stacks; use call numbers related to your topic to find the appropriate sections.

It is also wise to cultivate a librarian or two. Their knowledge and expertise can save you considerable time searching for information. Most librarians are willing to make appointments to help you create a search strategy, determine appropriate print and electronic databases for your research needs, and explain interlibrary loan services available to you. It is also a good idea to consult librarians about nontraditional sources on your topic, such as think tanks, professional associations, government documents, and publications from nonprofit organizations.

Do take time to explore other libraries and materials centers. You may be able to use regional college or university or special libraries near your home through consortia arrangements with your host university. You may also be able to purchase a library card to get access to another library; however, spend time doing an online search of the library's catalog for relevant resources before spending your money. Ask your local librarian to help you locate local libraries or information centers that may be relevant to your research.

Steps in Conducting a Literature Review

Conducting a thorough and scholarly review of the literature involves eight basic steps. The steps are not necessarily sequential; you will probably move back and forth between them.

Step 1: Identify key words or descriptors

Step 2: Create a search query

Step 3: Identify relevant literature sources

Step 4: Search the literature and collect relevant materials

Step 5: Critically read and analyze the literature

Step 6: Synthesize the literature

Step 7: Organize the literature

Step 8: Write the literature review

Step 1: Identify Key Words or Descriptors

Before beginning a search of the literature, it is important to develop a search strategy that effectively locates useful, relevant information. This involves identifying key words or descriptors to guide your review of the literature. Begin by creating a preliminary working title for your study that focuses you on what it is you want to know. Because it's a working title, it can always be revised. Also, state a central research question that describes the variables or concepts you need to examine in your literature review. Forcing yourself to write your topic as a single question requires you to bring it into clearer focus. Then, identify the key concepts in your title and central research question. The following are some examples:

- What effect does parental involvement have on the drop-out rate of bilingual middle school students?
- What are the differences between Mexicans and Mexican Americans in their perceptions of and feelings toward their pets?
- How does language use shape the identity of language-minority students?

Precise questions such as these help focus and guide the literature review. Depending on the complexity of your research, you may require several research questions to incorporate all of the variables or concepts you wish to examine in your dissertation. Also include alternative ways of phrasing and expressing concepts and ideas by consulting subject dictionaries and encyclopedias for the common terminology in your study area. Using an index or thesaurus is also advisable in order to establish useful terms. Various academic disciplines have their own thesauri. Some examples are *Thesaurus of ERIC Descriptors, Thesaurus of Psychological Index Terms,* and *Sociological Indexing Terms.* Fink (2010) described a thesaurus as "A controlled vocabulary that provides a consistent way to retrieve information across fields that may use different terms for the same concept" (p. 23).

From your research question(s) and working title, compile a list of key words, or descriptors, related to your topic.

Example:

What effect does parental involvement have on the drop-out rate of bilingual middle school students? Key words are

- parental involvement
- drop-out rate
- bilingual
- middle school students

Synonyms for parental involvement are *parent participation, mother involvement,* and *father involvement.* Synonyms for bilingual include *English as a second language* and *English language learners.*

> ### 💡 HELPFUL HINT
>
> Since you will be returning to the library time and again to continue your review, it is wise to develop a system of keeping track of which key words or descriptors you have checked in which volumes of which indexes. One effective way is to use a sheet of paper for each abstract or index you consult and create a matrix. Across the top, include the key words, or descriptors, you selected for that reference; down the left margin, list the dates of the volumes, starting with the most recent. As you go through each volume, place a check under the descriptors you used next to the date of the volume you used.

Step 2: Create a Search Query

Once you have identified your key words, you are ready to create a search query to use in the electronic databases. Using the example from Step 1, "What effect does parental involvement have on the drop-out rate of bilingual middle school students?" you would create a search query that looks like this:

("parental involvement" or "mother involvement" or "father involvement" or "parent participation") AND (dropout* or "drop out*") AND (bilingual or "English language learner*" or "English as a second language") and ("Middle school student*" or "junior high school student*")

Boolean Operators

Boolean operators define the relationships between words or groups of words. These commands to the database expand or limit your search by combining terms using the words AND, OR, or NOT. For example, to search for "What effect does alcohol have on college students' self-esteem?" type as your words: *alcohol, college students, self-esteem.*

- *AND* narrows the search by obtaining only those items with both Concept 1 and Concept 2 (*"college students" AND "self-esteem"*)
- *OR* broadens the search by obtaining all items with either Concept 1 or Concept 2 (*"self-esteem" OR "self-confidence"*).
- *NOT* obtains items with Concept 1 but eliminates those with Concept 2 (*"alcohol" NOT "illegal drugs"*)

Notice that multiword phrases were placed inside quotation marks. This is necessary to search those words in that order as a phrase. Remember to put phrases of two or more words in quotation marks.

Truncation

Through this process, you find variations of key words by adding a truncation symbol to the root. For example, to retrieve all variations on the root "psycholog" (i.e., to find *psychological, psychologist, psychology*), type Psycholog*
Truncation symbols vary with different databases (e.g., * ? $!).

Online Help

Instructions for using electronic databases are built into the system. Look for online help buttons or links such as "advanced search" and "search tips." Consult online help to learn

- How to enter searches
- What truncation symbol to use
- How to display results
- How to print or download records

Step 3: Identify Relevant Literature Sources

The best place to begin your search is with the databases and indexes in your academic area. They help you identify and locate research articles and other sources of information related to your research topic. A detailed description of available secondary sources is beyond the scope of this book. However, as an example, I list some major resources traditionally used by education and social science researchers. To find resources in your specific academic discipline, do a key word search in your university library's online catalog for your discipline (e.g., *sociology, psychology, anthropology*) followed by the word *handbook, encyclopedia, bibliography, thesaurus, dictionary, abstract, measures,* and so on. Also, consult with librarians at your university library or with faculty in your graduate program for resources they turn to when beginning a new research project.

In planning your search strategy, it is important to determine which academic disciplines are conducting research in your topic area. More than likely your research overlaps with other disciplines. For example: In the third research question in Step 1, "How does language use shape the identity of language-minority students?" you must decide what academic disciplines might conduct research on this topic. Possibilities include anthropology, psychology, education, communication, and sociology.

The following lists a variety of literature sources:

Selected Multidiscplinary Databases
Academic Search Premier (EbscoHost)
Communication and Mass Media (EbscoHost)
Research Library (ProQuest)
Social Sciences Citation Index (Web of Science)
Wilson OmniFile (H. W. Wilson)
Selected Anthropology Databases
Anthropology Plus (FirstSearch)
AnthroSource (American Anthropological Association)
Anthropological Index Online (Royal Anthropological Institute)
Sociological Abstracts (Cambridge Scientific Abstracts)
Selected Education Databases
Education Resources Information Center (ERIC): *http://eric.ed.gov/*
Education Research Complete (EbscoHost)
Education Full-Text (H. W. Wilson)
ProQuest Education (ProQuest)
Selected Psychology Databases
PsycArticles (American Psychological Association)
PsycInfo (American Psychological Association)

ProQuest Psychology (ProQuest)
Psychology and Behavioral Sciences Collection (EbscoHost)
Selected Sociology Databases
Sociological Abstracts (Cambridge Scientific Abstracts)
SocIndex With Full-Text (EbscoHost)
Social Sciences Index (H.W. Wilson)
Social Sciences Citation Index (Web of Science)
Social Services Abstracts (Cambridge Scientific Abstracts)
Bibliographies, Encyclopedias, and Dictionaries
Biographical Dictionary of Social and Cultural Anthropology
Cambridge Dictionary of Sociology
Corsini Encyclopedia of Psychology and Behavioral Science
Encyclopedia of Education
Encyclopedia of Leadership
Handbooks and Reviews of Research Literature
Bass and Stogdill's Handbook of Leadership
Handbook of Research on the Education of Young Children
Handbook of Research in Emotional and Behavioral Disorders
The Handbook of Research on Teaching
Handbook of School Psychology
Dissertations
American Doctoral Dissertations (print)
Dissertation Abstracts International (print)
Index to Tests Used in Educational Dissertations by Emily Fabiano
ProQuest Dissertations & Theses Database (ProQuest)
Literature Related to Published and Unpublished Measures
Published Measures (Reviews of Instruments)
ETS TestLink

(Continued)

(Continued)

(www.ets.org/portal/site/ets/menuitem.1488512ecfd5b8849a77b13bc3921509/?vgnext oid=ed462d3631df4010VgnVCM10000022f95190RCRD&vgnextchannel=85af197a484f40 10VgnVCM10000022f95190RCRD)
Mental Measurement Yearbook (http://buros.unl.edu/buros/jsp/search.jsp) Free searching, but charges to see review—also available full text from vendors such as EbscoHost
PRO-ED Test Review
Tests in Print
Unpublished Measures (Sample Instruments)
Assessments A to Z: A collection of 50 Questionnaires, Instruments, and Inventories
Handbook of Family Measurement Techniques (vol. 3)
Handbook of Organizational Measurement
Handbook of Tests and Measurement in Education and the Social Sciences
Measures for Clinical Practice
Scales for the Measurement of Attitudes
These are only a few sources of measurement available. Check with your library and the Internet under your specific academic discipline.
Books
Ebrary (full text electronic books available through subscription by your library)
Google Book Search (http://books.google.com/books?um=1&q=&btnG=Search+Books)
NetLibrary (full text electronic books available through subscription by your library)
Project Gutenberg (www.gutenberg.org/wiki/Main_Page)
WorldCat (catalog of library holdings worldwide) (www.worldcat.org)
Grey Literature
Grey literature is literature not available through published databases or indexes. It can be in print and electronic formats. These are documents published by governmental agencies, academic institutions, corporations, research centers, professional organizations, and so on. Some examples are • Working papers • Technical reports • Government documents

- Government documents
- Conference or symposia proceedings
- White papers
- Business documents
- Newsletters
- Monographs
- Letters and diaries

While these are not scholarly documents, they can provide up-to-date facts and statistics to broaden knowledge about a particular topic. The downside is that they are often difficult to find, and they must be carefully evaluated as they are not peer reviewed. One way to locate grey literature is to search the agency or institution that produces the literature; another way is to consult a librarian. For a thorough explanation of grey literature and how to find it, refer to *Doing a Literature Search* by Chris Hart (2004), Chapters 7 and 8. You will also find a selection of web-based resources in grey literature at Grey Literature Network Service (www.greynet.org).

Existing Literature Review and Systematic Literature Review Articles

These articles, including meta-analysis and meta-synthesis, consist solely of a literature review and are invaluable sources of data. They provide a good overview of research that has been conducted by synthesizing findings from individual studies. Many peer-reviewed systematic reviews are available in journals as well as from databases and other electronic sources. The bibliographic references are also very helpful.

Additional Useful Sources

American Educational Research Association (www.aera.net)

U. S. Deparment of Education (www.ed.gov)

WestEd (www.wested.org)

U.S. Regional Educational Laboratories (http://ies.ed.gov/ncee/edlabs)

Locating Statistics (www.FedStats.gov)

United States Government Printing Office (www.gpo.gov)

Step 4: Search the Literature and Collect Relevant Materials

Begin your search for relevant literature by searching the databases, indexes, books, and other sources listed in Step 3. Examine your results. Are the materials you are finding relevant? Do you see other key words you could add or subtract from your search? Do particular authors seem to be conducting research on this topic? Do particular journals seem to be publishing research in this area? Use this information to help you focus your search.

When searching the Internet for literature, remember that some information may not be dependable, meaning it has not passed the standards of peer reviewers—journal editors or book publishers. Creswell (2008) elaborated this point by stating, "Material obtained from Web sites not in national, refereed journals needs to be carefully screened to determine the qualifications of the author, the quality of the writing, and the scope and rigor of data collection and analysis" (p. 104). For additional information on evaluating websites, please see Chapter 8 in this book.

Once you have reviewed the list of references located in your database searches, the next step is to determine which books and articles are most relevant to your study and collect each primary source. Primary source documents contain the original work of researchers and authors. As a serious researcher, you should not rely solely on secondary sources. They do not always provide reliable information. Secondary sources interpret, analyze, or summarize primary sources. They include such published works as newspapers, encyclopedias, handbooks, conference proceedings, and so on. Your review should be based on primary sources whenever possible.

Collecting primary literature consists of browsing, skimming, reading, and photocopying books and documents related to your study. Two types of literature you should collect for your review are the theoretical literature and the research literature. Since most dissertations have a theoretical base, you need to be familiar with those conceptual areas related to your study. In addition, you must be thoroughly familiar with previous research in your subject area.

Collecting literature is an ongoing process, and you need some mechanism for classifying it into those that have a direct bearing on your topic and those that bear generally on your topic. Since it is not feasible to collect all the titles yielded in your search of secondary sources, you must be selective and choose only those most relevant to your study. Always keep in mind your study's purpose. As you gather and sort documents, ask yourself, How does this relate to my problem? One strategy is to categorize each book or article as either *very important*, *moderately important*, or *somewhat important* to your study. If you took the time to familiarize yourself with the library, locating and obtaining documents will be considerably more efficient.

Keeping Track of Pertinent Documents: Organizing Strategies

It is helpful to keep a record of each book or document you consult. With so many to read, you can easily lose track of those already reviewed. You should prepare bibliographic citations for each. One simple way is to list the bibliographic information on index cards and keep them arranged alphabetically by the last name of the author. Another way is to simply maintain an ongoing record of the bibliographic data in your computer. Reference management software programs you download to your computer, such as EndNote, ProCite, Connotea, and Zotero, enable you to create a list of citations, and they automatically convert them into the appropriate style format. The newest release of Microsoft Word 2007 also allows users to choose a citation style format, such as APA. Reference management databases, such as RefWorks, store your citations on their server and allow you to access your records from any computer that has access to the Internet. Check with your library or your graduate program to see which programs they provide or support.

At this point, you must decide on the specific bibliographic style you plan to use in your dissertation. I recommend that you consult with your advisor on this issue. Many of them have preferred styles of citation.

A second organizing strategy is to develop a two-dimensional matrix in which you identify the variables or key descriptors in each publication you consult. To do this, list your variables or descriptors across the top of the page. Then, down the left-hand side of the page, list each reference and its publication date. You can then place a check mark where the variable and reference intersect. Following is an example of this matrix.

Figure 9.1	Example: Principles of Effective Professional Development Frequency of Reference

Name	A	B	C	D	E	F	G	Etc.
Arpin, Krant, 1991							X	
Betaini, Tafel, 1989			X	X	X	X		
Castle, 1989				X				
Fullan, 1991		X	X	X	X	X	X	
Garmston, 1991		X	X		X		X	
Etc.								
Total		16	9	9	11	15	12	

SOURCE: Nevills (1995).

NOTE: The letters at the top of the table represent the principles of effective professional development that were identified through a literature review. The total indicates the frequency with which each item appeared.

A = Adults as learners; B = Self-directing; C = Practical, relevant; D = Involved in planning; E = Evaluation and assessment; F = Focus on needs and concerns; G = Mentoring feedback; etc.

This matrix provides a graphic portrayal of the variables or concepts most frequently discussed in the literature. Not only does this process help you keep track of your reading in the literature, it helps you initially select your variables and key concepts you might wish to study. It also is a good mechanism for developing your research instruments.

A variation of this organizing strategy is the author-subtopic matrix in which you note the specific pages on which subtopic information can be located. This is accomplished by putting the page numbers across from the subtopic and under the correct author. For example:

Authors			
Subtopics	McClellan, 1980	Hersey/Blanchard, 1988	Yuki, 1989
Sources of Power	p. 280	p. 204	p. 14
Charisma, etc.		p. 218	p. 204

After locating pertinent articles for review, you should download the full text to your computer's hard drive or to a portable storage device such as a jump drive or external hard drive. If the articles are in a print journal, photocopy them to read at a more convenient time. I suggest you make a complete photocopy of all articles central to your topic, especially those you want to cite.

Dissertations directly relating to your study can be purchased from Proquest's Dissertation Express (www.proquest.com/products_umi/dissertations/disexpress.shtml). Before purchasing, check with your university library; the full text of dissertations may be available to you at no additional charge through the ProQuest Dissertations & Theses database. Other dissertations not available in the library might be obtained through the interlibrary loan process.

Step 5: Critically Read and Analyze the Literature

While collecting your literature, it is necessary to read it critically. This involves questioning, speculating, evaluating, thinking through, and analyzing what you read. What original insights can you gather about your topic that are not stated in any of the references? What important facts and opinions relate to your study? Are there important issues that are not well addressed? You must be able to evaluate and integrate the material you read.

Noting and Summarizing References

1. *Do an in-depth reading of your* very important *publications first so you can understand them thoroughly.* Highlight important parts and

write down any ideas, insights, or questions that come to you while reading. You can also write on sticky notes or make notations in the margins.

2. *For every book or article you read, write a brief summary in your own words that illustrates the essential points.* Also include inferences you can make about your study and conclusions you can draw from the book or article.

3. *Be sure to accurately record the bibliographic reference exactly as it will appear in the final reference list placed in the dissertation.* Include the library call number if it is a book.

4. *Develop a coding system so you can identify the type of materials contained on each summary sheet.* Usually, this is done by your variables, key topics, or by the descriptors used in locating the references. Write the name at the top of the sheet.

5. *As you are reading, be alert for quotations that might be useful in presenting your review.* If you find quotable material, be sure to copy it carefully with the quotation marks and include the page from which it was taken. Including quotation marks helps you remember which statements are direct quotations. You do not want to inadvertently plagiarize others' ideas. Too often, students overuse quotations in their dissertations. A good rule of thumb for determining whether or not to directly quote an author was provided by Borg and Gall (1983). They said to quote "only materials that are stated very skillfully, or in very concise terms, or are typical and clear reflections of a particular point of view the student wishes to illustrate" (pp. 182–183). *Try to limit the number of direct quotations.*

6. *Place your summaries in a computer file and then print it out, leaving wide margins.* You now have a complete record of what the literature stated about the variables or key concepts in your study.

7. *Read through your summaries and look for important themes, big issues, commonalities, and differences.* Make notations in the margins of your summary sheets. This provides the basis for developing a logical, coherent outline.

A technique that can be used in preparation for synthesis writing is to *build tables to summarize the literature,* a technique promoted by Galvan (2006). He believes that building tables is an effective way to overview, organize, and summarize the literature. In his book, *Writing Literature Reviews,* Galvan (2006) provided examples on how to build summary tables such as a table of definitions and key terms and concepts, a table of research methods, a table of research results, or a table that summarizes theories relevant to your study. Other tables could summarize related quantitative or qualitative studies. Many kinds of tables can be developed to help you get a comprehensive overview of the literature, which is quite useful in the early stages of synthesizing literature.

Step 6: Synthesize the Literature

After you have critically read and analyzed the collected literature, it is time to synthesize the ideas and information that was gathered. Synthesizing involves comparing, contrasting, and merging disparate pieces of information into one coherent whole that provides a new perspective. This works much like a jigsaw puzzle: The individual pieces of information are placed into a new whole, creating an original work. Critical synthesis is most difficult for students to achieve. Too often, students discuss the literature as a chain of isolated summaries of previous studies, such as "White says . . ."; "Smith found . . ."; "French concluded . . ." with no attempt to explain the relationship among them or to compare what is being studied. Like individual beads on a necklace, they string together a series of annotations that describe the current state of knowledge about the study but fail to organize the material. This reflects a shotgun approach and misses the point of an integrated literature review. Remember, books and articles are not bricks with mortar banding them together. You need to create the mortar.

A high-quality literature review reflects careful analysis of all sources and a critical synthesis in which you show how previous studies and information are related to each other and to your study. Describing trees represents the analysis process; describing the forest is the synthesis process and involves "creating a unique new forest" (Galvan, 2006, p. 72). You synthesize the literature when you

- Identify relationships among studies (such as which ones were landmark studies leading to subsequent studies)
- Compare (show commonalities) and contrast (show differences) the works, ideas, theories, or concepts from various authors
- Comment on the major themes and patterns you discovered
- Show evidence of common results using data from multiple sources
- Discuss the pros and cons of the issues
- Explain a conflict or contradiction among different sources
- Point out gaps in the literature, reflecting on why these exist based on the understandings you gained in reading in your study area
- Note inconsistencies across studies over time
- Make generalizations across studies

- Discuss how and why ideas about your topic have changed over time
- Make connections between the sources cited
- Discuss literature that has a direct bearing on your area of study

Before you can write a good synthesis, however, you must first recognize the main points and key ideas of the sources you use. Then, as you read through your written summaries, identify the major themes, trends, or patterns and the big issues, commonalities, and differences among the different authors, and identify your own insights that go beyond what anyone else said. When you do this, you bring your own voice forward rather than that of the authors cited. After all, this is your study and, therefore, it is your responsibility to make sense of the literature to help readers see the information and your topic in a new way and in greater depth. The bottom line is to critique the literature; don't duplicate it. This sounds easier than it is, for rarely are these trends, patterns, and so on spelled out in the literature. They become apparent to you as you develop insight into the big picture that emerged over time.

Techniques for Synthesizing the Literature

Various techniques can be used to synthesize the literature. This section provides an overview of some of these techniques. One useful technique I use with doctoral students is a *synthesis matrix*. A synthesis matrix chart identifies themes and patterns or arguments across sources. The top of the matrix lists the various sources of comparison (by author or article), and the side represents the common themes, arguments, or main ideas identified in the articles. See Figure 9.2.

Figure 9.2 Visionary Leadership Synthesis Matrix

Common Themes	Source 1	Source 2	Source 3	Source 4	Source 5
Vision is a key element in both charismatic and transformational leadership theories	•		•		
The visioning process includes at least two stages: creating the vision and communicating the vision		•			•
Visions are best developed collaboratively	•		•	•	

(Continued)

| Figure 9.2 | (Continued) |

Common Themes	Source 1	Source 2	Source 3	Source 4	Source 5
Definitions of vision include the ideas of providing direction and purpose	•		•		•
Vision seems vital to an organization's success		•			
The outcome of visions is commitment			•		•
Metaphors used 1. "Glue" that holds the school together Etc.	•			•	

A synthesis matrix such as this helps you begin to link studies together and identify the themes and patterns that appear across your literature sources.

Another useful technique for synthesis writing is to *bring your own voice to the foreground.* According to Ridley (2008), this means presenting your own voice assertively by "taking control of the text and leading your reader through the content. This can be done by making your own assertions with appropriate citations to provide support, and by including explicit linking words and phrases to show connections between citations and the different sections and chapters in the text" (p. 131). Ridley's book, *The Literature Review: A Step-by-Step Guide for Students,* provides rich examples on how to use language and citations to foreground your own voice in writing your literature review.

Constructing a "literature map" is an idea promoted by Creswell (2009) in his book, *Research Design: Qualitative, Quantitative, and Mixed Methods Approaches.* This technique provides a visual summary of the literature—a figure or drawing. Not only does this technique provide an overview of the existing literature, it also "helps you see overlaps in information or major topics in the literature and can help you determine how a proposed study adds to or extends the existing literature rather than duplicates past studies" (Creswell, 2009, p. 107).

You could also create a summary chart of the literature using a concept mapping program such as Inspiration (free 30-day trial download available at www.inspiration.com). A concept map is a diagram showing the relationships among concepts. Concepts, usually represented as boxes or circles, are connected with labeled arrows in a downward-branching hierarchical structure revealing relationships and patterns among concepts.

Step 7: Organize the Literature

Once analysis and synthesis of the literature are complete, you must consider how your review will be organized and written. Of primary importance is that your review be structured in a logical and coherent manner. Too often, discussions of related literature are disorganized ramblings. There is no design, no structure that organizes and integrates the material discussed. Following are some guidelines for organizing your review:

Select an Organizational Framework

Prior to writing your first draft, you need to decide on an organizational structure for your review. There are a variety of organizational principles to organize and structure your literature review. Below are some commonly used in social science research.

a. *Chronological*—the "acorn to oak" approach. Organizing your review chronologically means that you group and discuss your sources in order of their appearance (usually publication), highlighting the emergence of a topic over a period of time. This approach is useful for historical research or other studies where time is an important element.

b. *Thematic*—the "four schools of thought . . ." or "six themes that emerge . . ." approach. Organizing your review thematically means discussing your sources in terms of themes, topics, important concepts, or major issues. This approach integrates the literature and depends on your ability to synthesize information effectively.

c. *General to Specific*—the "V" or "funnel" approach. First, discuss general material to provide a comprehensive perspective. Last, discuss material most closely related to your study. Rudestam and Newton (2007) used the metaphor of filmmaking to explain this approach. They discussed "long shots and close ups" to display the degrees of depth required relative to the closeness and relevance of the literature to your study. *Long shots* refer to a topic's background information and are described more generally. *Medium shots* are those sources more closely related to your study and are critiqued in more detail. *Close-ups* refer to those sources with direct bearing on your study, thus requiring a more critical examination.

Create a Topic Outline

If you want your review to be coherent, logical, and well organized, create a topic outline. It helps to do this prior to writing; however, don't be surprised if it changes as you write. In writing your outline, first list the main topics and the order in which they should be presented. Then, under each heading determine the logical subheadings. Adding additional subheadings depends on the complexity of your problem. The outline helps you see headings that need rearranging to create a logical flow of thought. Following is an example of a partial topic outline from a dissertation.

EXAMPLE: REVIEW OF THE LITERATURE

Topical Outline

A Case Study of the Perceived Characteristics and Life Events

That Enabled Four Women to Become University Presidents

I. Introduction

    A. Focus on women college presidents

    B. Overview of the areas to be covered

    C. Restatement of the purpose of the study and its importance

II. Affirmative Action

    A. Women's participation in higher education

    B. Discrimination in access to education and employment

    C. Legislative changes; women and underrepresented groups

III. Networks and Training Opportunities

    A. Early studies about the status of women in education

    B. Identification of women leaders and the development of networks

IV. Status of Women in Higher Education Administration

    A. Lack of women presidents

    B. Studies of women executives in higher education

        1. Degrees attained

        2. Age

        3. Religious affiliation

        4. Marital status

        5. Career ladders

SOURCE: Cooper (1992).

With a completed outline, you can sort your references under their appropriate subheadings. Then you must decide in which order the headings should be presented. It is a challenging task to combine and interpret the literature into a well-organized and unified picture of the state of knowledge in your area.

> **HELPFUL HINT**
>
> Obtain a 9″ × 12″ box in which you can hang file folders. Then, create a file folder for each heading and subheading in your outline. Insert the articles and notes related to each in the folder. The advantage of putting them in a box rather than a file cabinet is that you can keep it near your computer at all times, and you can carry it with you if necessary.

Step 8: Write the Literature Review

Pretend your literature review is a discussion with a friend regarding what authors have written about your problem area. Basically, your review is an informative "story" of what is known about your topic—a summary of the state of the art. You should write for an audience who is intelligent but not knowledgeable about your study. This means limiting as much as possible jargon and specialized nomenclature.

Style Manuals

Most universities require consistent use of a particular style manual to format your dissertation document and to cite references. Those widely used in the social sciences are the following:

American Anthropological Association. (2003). *AAA style guide.* Retrieved from www.aaanet.org/publications/style_guide.pdf

American Psychological Association. (2010). *Publication manual of the American Psychological Association* (6th ed.). Washington, DC: American Psychological Association.

American Psychological Association. (2007). *APA style guide to electronic resources.* Available from http://books.apa.org/books.cfm?id=4210509

American Sociological Association. (1997). *ASA style guide* (2nd ed.). Washington, DC: American Sociological Association.

American Sociological Association. (2008). *A quick style guide for students writing sociology papers.* Retrieved August 18, 2008 from www.asanet.org/page.ww?name=Quick+Style+Guide&section=Sociology+Depts

Gibaldi, J. (2003). *MLA handbook for writers of research papers* (6th ed.). New York: Modern Language Association of America.

Lipson, C. (2006). *Cite right: A quick guide to citation styles—MLA, APA, Chicago, the sciences, professions, and more.* Chicago: University of Chicago Press.

Modern Language Association. (2008). *MLA style manual and guide to scholarly publishing* (3rd ed.). New York: Modern Language Association of America.

Turabian, K. L. (2007). *A manual for writers of term papers, theses, and dissertations: Chicago style for students and researchers* (7th ed.). Chicago: University of Chicago Press.

University of Chicago. (2003). *The Chicago manual of style: The essential guide for writers, editors, and publishers* (15th ed.). Chicago: University of Chicago Press.

I highly recommend that you become familiar with your required style manual and begin using it consistently in writing your literature review as well as other sections of your dissertation. It's not as easy as it seems to learn the nuances of headings, in-text citations, end-of-text references, footnotes, and tables and figures. Mastering these techniques early saves you considerable time and effort in the long run.

Techniques for Writing the Literature Review

Typically, a review of the literature begins with a brief introduction that tells about the presentation of your literature review—what it is about, the scope, and the organizational structure you selected. Following the introduction, present the various sections where you review and synthesize the literature. For each subsection, write an introduction and then describe the information and relevant studies. For example:

> This section is organized chronologically to provide a perspective of trends in the formal evaluation of school superintendents.

Use Headings and Subheadings

This helps the reader follow your train of thought. Usually, headings reflect your study's major variables or themes found in the literature.

Employ Summary Tables

Where considerable research exists, summary tables help cut through a huge mass of literature. Such a table might look like the following:

Research on Cognitive Coaching Classroom		
	Subjects	Results
Garmston & Hyerle (1988)	Eight university professors of mathematics, geology, communications studies, school administration, counseling, and theater arts in a peer coaching cognitive coaching project	Maximally effective at producing increased confidence about enthusiasm for teaching

SOURCE: Costa & Garmston (1994).

You can modify this table format by including other topics of comparison such as methodology or conclusions.

Use Transition Phrases

Such phrases guide the reader from one paragraph to the next. It is important that you make strong connections between what has already been reviewed and the material that follows.

Summarize

Pull together each major section with a brief summary at the end. Summaries highlight and clarify the main points of a section, especially if it is long and complex. Conclude by highlighting and summarizing the key points made throughout the literature review.

Emphasize Relatedness

Remember to link studies together by comparing the similarities and differences among them. To keep from boring the reader, be sure to use transitions to integrate paragraphs.

If several studies say essentially the same thing, it is not necessary to describe each one. You can make a summary statement followed by all the related references, for example, "Several studies have found . . . (Brown, 2007; Jones, 2008; Smith, 2006)." Be careful not to ignore studies that contradict other studies. You may evaluate them and try to figure out a plausible explanation, for example, "Contrary to these studies is the work of Smith and Jones (1998), who found. . . ."

Advice on Writing a Literature Review

1. Be Thorough

Include both computer and hand searches; avoid shortcuts. You must cover the full scope of the field. A solid literature review establishes you as an expert and provides a strong background to your research effort.

2. Write With Authority

You are in charge of your literature review, so develop a critical perspective in discussing others' work. Cite relevant authors to emphasize *your* argument or to provide notable examples of the point *you* are making. Don't start a paragraph with someone else's name; rather, start each paragraph with the point you wish to make followed by studies and examples that illustrate and enhance your point.

3. Critique Rather Than Just Report the Literature

You must evaluate and integrate the material you read. Compare and contrast the various studies related to your problem. Comment on the major themes and issues you discovered. In other words, bring meaning to the literature you review; don't just review what has been reported.

4. Avoid Excessive Use of Quotations

Use quotations only when the material quoted is impactful, stated in a unique way, or can be inserted without impairing the continuity of your writing. An accumulation of quotations linked by a sentence or two results in a review that is disjointed and difficult to read.

5. Be Selective

Avoid the temptation to report everything you read. A literature review is not a collection of every book and article relating to a topic. Include only material directly related to your study's purpose and the necessary background to your variables. All the books and articles you read were necessary to help you become an expert in your study area. Like in a courtroom, all the admissible evidence presented must pertain directly to the case and question at hand.

6. Be Careful Not to Plagiarize

To *plagiarize* is "to steal and pass off the ideas and words of another as one's own without crediting the source . . . to commit literary theft" (Webster's Collegiate Dictionary, Tenth Edition, p. 888). Using someone else's words without quotation marks, closely paraphrasing others' sentences, and stating others' ideas as if they were yours are all forms of plagiarism. Remember to always acknowledge another's ideas whenever you cite or borrow them.

7. Critique the Literature; Don't Duplicate It

It is your job to organize and summarize references in a meaningful way. Don't quote long passages or cite at length others' ideas and words. First, present your own review followed by a paraphrase or short, direct quotations. Use long quotations only for good reason.

8. Use Primary Sources

Primary sources give you information "straight from the horse's mouth." They are preferable to secondary sources that are the interpretation of another's work. Find the original books and articles and read them yourself. If you cannot locate the original source, then follow your style manual's guidelines for citing secondary sources. "References to the work of one author as quoted in that of another must cite both works" (Turabian, 1996, p. 163). Following is a literature review checklist to assess the quality and thoroughness of your literature review.

Literature Review Checklist

After writing the first draft of the literature review, use the following checklist to assess the thoroughness and quality of what you wrote. Before sending it to your advisor, ask a critical friend to read and comment on your review. Your advisor will be eternally grateful! A well-thought-out, well-written, and interesting review of the literature is a joy to read.

Please note that the items in this checklist comprise a generic set of "to dos" when designing a literature review. Not all the items are relevant for all reviews. Select only those that fit your particular situation, and use them as a guide.

_____ The literature review is comprehensive (covers the major points of the topic).

_____ There is balanced coverage of all variables in the study.

_____ The review is well organized. It flows logically. It is not fragmented.

_____ The writer critically analyzes the literature rather than stringing together a series of citations.

_____ There is a logical correspondence between the Introduction chapter and the Literature Review.

_____ At least three-fourths of the review focuses on the variables or concepts identified in the purpose statement and research questions. The remaining one-fourth sets the stage and gives the big picture and background to the study.

_____ For each variable or concept, there is some historical and current coverage; the emphasis is on current coverage.

_____ The review relies on empirical research studies, not opinion articles in "pop" journals.

_____ The review contains opposing points of view (especially if the researcher has a strong bias).

_____ There is a summary at the end of each major section as well as at the end of the chapter.

_____ The bibliography contains at least 40 to 60 references.

_____ The majority of references were published within the past 5 years.

_____ Primary sources are used in the majority of citations.

_____ There is an appropriate amount of paraphrasing and direct quotation.

_____ The direct quotations do not detract from the readability of the chapter.

_____ Authors who make the same point are combined in the citation.

_____ The review synthesizes and integrates meaning to the literature; it is not just a catalog of sources.

Summary

It is important to read and analyze the literature surrounding your study as early as possible in the dissertation process. To do this efficiently, you should thoroughly familiarize yourself with the library and its various search tools. There are eight basic steps for conducting a literature review:

1. Identify keywords or descriptors
2. Create a search query
3. Identify relevant literature sources
4. Search the literature and collect relevant materials
5. Critically read and analyze the literature
6. Synthesize the literature
7. Organize the literature
8. Write the literature review

Presenting the results of a literature review is a challenging task. To create a well-organized and integrated review, you should first create a topic outline to help provide a logical flow of thought. In presenting the review, employ techniques such as headings and subheadings, summary tables, transition phrases, and summaries. It is important that you critique and bring meaning to the literature rather than just report what others say.

The next chapter focuses on the writing phase. It offers you some important tips for attaining a strong, vigorous, and scholarly writing style.

10

Mastering the Academic Style

Anyone who wishes to become a good writer should endeavor, before he allows himself to be tempted by the more showy qualities, to be direct, simple, brief, vigorous, and lucid.

—Fowler and Fowler, *The King's English*

Qualities of Scholarly Writing

The qualities espoused by Fowler and Fowler in the opening quote represent the heart and soul of good expository writing. However, two additional qualities define the scholarly, academic writing required for dissertation writing: *precision* and *logic*. Knowing how to express your ideas in logical sequence and in a clear and concise manner is critical to your success as a scholarly practitioner. The qualities of logic, precision, clarity, directness, and brevity are also qualities of effective thinking. Zinsser (1994) stated, "Writing is thinking on paper. . . . If you can think clearly about the things you know and care about, you can write—with confidence and enjoyment" (p. vii).

Every dissertation advisor I know would affirm that scholarly writing is impossible without clear, logical, and precise thinking. There is a close and reciprocal relationship between good writing and clear thinking. Since writing is a reflection of thinking, the quality of your writing depends on how well you think. Clear, logical thinking usually precedes writing; however, the act of writing clarifies your thinking and develops logical thought. This is why many dissertation advisors, rather than endlessly discussing your dissertation, say, "Put it in writing and then we can discuss it."

To be able to express yourself clearly, logically, and with precision, you must be in command of basic writing skills such as constructing grammatical sentences, using appropriate transitions, and remaining focused and concise. If you have difficulty expressing yourself clearly, I strongly suggest that you hire an editor early on to assist you with the writing process. Your committee should not have to spend its time editing or teaching you basic composition skills.

Even if you write reasonably well, you may, like most students, initially experience difficulty writing in the scholarly, academic style required for dissertations. This can be verified by many dissertation advisors who received drafts of dissertation chapters that could be classified as clumsy, muddled, and verbose. Reading such writing is tortuous and dulls the senses. The better you write, the fewer revisions you will make and the sooner you will obtain those three signatures required for graduation.

The good news is that this kind of writing can be learned. You don't need inspiration, just a good dose of determination, perseverance, and patience. These three characteristics usually can overcome any lack of innate talent. There are many excellent books with good advice on improving your writing. However, the best way to learn to write more effectively is to write a lot, obtain feedback on your writing, and rewrite.

For most people, writing is a difficult, complex, and laborious task requiring self-discipline and mental concentration to stay the course for any length of time. As a doctoral student, you have the extra burden of knowing that your document will be open to public scrutiny and judgment, first to your committee and then to the academic community at large. Your reputation as a scholar and that of your committee are at stake when your dissertation is signed and printed.

This section presents guidelines and tips to help you understand some of the critical elements that contribute to scholarly writing. It incorporates key thoughts on writing from a variety of sources plus my own experience in guiding students in writing academic papers and dissertations.

This book cannot begin to cover the myriad topics devoted to improving the writing process. Instead, I focus on my observations and those of my colleagues as to the major errors made by doctoral students in writing their papers and dissertations. I also include information about effective writing from noted authorities in the field. The following section identifies some common writing problems, followed by eight tips for good writing.

> What is written without effort is, in general, read without pleasure.
>
> —Samuel Johnson

Common Writing Problems

I asked a group of dissertation advisors to respond to the question, "What are the most common writing problems you see while guiding dissertation students?" Their responses revolved around four major areas: organization, paragraphs, sentence construction, and direct quotations. Following summarizes their responses:

Organization

- Rambling in literature review
- Failure to develop ideas in a logical sequence
- Problem statements that are "all over the wall"
- Lack of organization
- Lack of consistency
- Failure to use headings
- Inappropriate use of the required style manual
- Little evidence of proofreading

Paragraphs

- One-sentence paragraphs
- Unclear antecedent for *this*
- Paragraphs not developed as a clear center of thought
- Lack of transitions
- Weak transitions
- Failure to indicate where the paragraph is going—"bones without a skeleton"
- Introducing a topic and then failing to discuss the topic
- Lack of details that are explicit and related to the main idea
- Paragraphs that lack focus

Sentence Construction

- Overlong sentences
- Subject-verb agreement (e.g., *data were* is correct, not *data was*)

Direct Quotations

- Inappropriate use of direct quotations
- Excessive quoting

The following section offers some tips to help overcome these writing problems and others encountered in the writing process.

Tips for Good Writing

Tip 1: Write in a Conversational Tone

Do your best to write naturally, as if you were conversing with an intelligent person unfamiliar with your topic. When you do this, your writing takes on the energy and liveliness of good conversation. So often students believe they must write in a formal, stilted, grandiose manner quite different from the way they talk. There is artificiality about this kind of writing that makes it boring and tedious for readers. People prefer reading simple, understandable writing.

Tip 2: Trim Excess Words

Say what you need to say in as few words as possible, using the simplest language. Strunk and White (1979) stated this idea clearly:

> Vigorous writing is concise. A sentence should contain no unnecessary words, a paragraph no unnecessary sentences, for the same reason that a drawing should have no unnecessary lines and a machine no unnecessary parts. This requires not that the writer make all his sentences short, or that he avoid all detail and treat his subjects only in outline, but that every word tell. (p. 23)

Strunk and White (1979, p. 24) provided some commonly used phrases that violate conciseness, along with some briefer options:

he is a man who	he
this is a subject that	this subject
the reason why that is	because
owing to the fact that	since

Preposition Alert!

Another example of verbosity includes the overuse of prepositions (e.g., *by, under, because, of, for, with*). Good writing is clear, concise, and interesting. Overusing prepositions creates the opposite of that; it causes wordy writing—boring and hard to understand. It's so much easier to drop in preposition after preposition than to find active verbs that keep your writing powerful and interesting. Preposition overuse is a common writing fault that can be easily corrected. Munter (1997) offered a technique to overcome this habit. She suggested "circling, or having a computer program highlight, all the prepositions in a sample page of your writing. If you consistently find more than four in a sentence, you need to revise and shorten. 'Of' is usually the worst offender" (p. 70). So help trim excess words in your writing by eliminating overuse of prepositions and their wordy baggage.

Additional culprits to avoid are the compound prepositional phrase and verbs with prepositions. Following is a list of common compound prepositional phrases and verbs with prepositions and their more concise counterparts:

1. Compound Prepositional Phrase	Write
with reference to, with regard/ respect to	about, concerning
by reason of	because
during the course of	during
in close proximity to	near
in order to	to
2. Verbs With Prepositions	**Write**
make an examination of	examine
perform an analysis of	analyze
make assumptions about	assume
give consideration to	consider
is dependent on	depends on

Qualifiers

It is also important to trim little qualifiers from your writing. Words that say how you feel and think dilute the forcefulness and persuasiveness of your writing. Examples of such qualifiers are *sort of, kind of, quite, very, too,* and *a little.*

Tip 3: Use Short Sentences Rather Than Long

Long, complex sentences filled with convoluted phrases and multiple clauses are obstacles to easy reading. Trying to decipher such writing drains your readers' energy and interest. Don't be afraid to break long sentences into two or more shorter sentences. Munter (1997) offered three options for breaking up long sentences:

1. Break into three sentences using transitions: first, second . . .

2. Break up long sentences with internal enumeration: (1), (2) . . .

3. Break up long sentences with bullet points

Remember, each sentence should contain *one thought and one thought only.*

Tip 4: Write Clear, Well-Constructed Paragraphs

A well-constructed paragraph organizes your thoughts coherently. Create paragraphs that contain only one main idea. Usually, the main idea is expressed as a topic sentence at the beginning of the paragraph. It is helpful to begin each paragraph with a topic sentence followed by supporting sentences that illustrate, explain, or clarify your main point. Supporting information might include a specific fact, statistic, direct quotation, anecdote, and so on. Be sure not to write extra-long paragraphs because they are overwhelming to readers. Also, don't write single sentences as paragraphs. Murray (1995) reminded us to use the old-fashioned "CUE" method to develop paragraphs:

Coherence. One thing should logically lead to the next

Unity. Everything in the paragraph should be about one thing

Emphasis. The main point of the paragraph should be clear (p. 205)

Remember to pay particular attention to the last sentence of each paragraph, for it's the critical springboard to the following paragraph.

Tip 5: Use the Active Voice

Whenever possible, use the active voice in your writing. Active verbs give vitality to your writing. "The active voice is usually more direct and vigorous than the passive . . . and makes for forcible writing" (Strunk & White, 1979, p. 18). The following examples contrast the passive and active voices:

Passive: This paper was written by me.

Active: *I wrote the paper.*

Passive: The nurse is supervisor of the health program.

Active: *The nurse supervises the health program.*

Passive: The advisor was hesitant to approve the research design.

Active: *The advisor hesitated to approve the design.*

Passive: The dissertation will be edited by members of the committee.

Active: *The committee will edit the dissertation.*

One sign of the passive voice is the use of linking verbs such as *was, will be, have been,* and *is.* Sentences containing any form of the verb *to be* are eligible for rewriting in active voice. Circle all the linking verbs in your own writing or have a computer highlight them. You will find that "75 percent of them can be eliminated" (Munter, 1997, p. 69). Write as straightforwardly as you can, using strong verbs—not ones that lack action (*is, was*, etc.).

The choice between using the active or passive voice in writing is a matter of style, not correctness. There is nothing inherently wrong with the passive voice, but if you can say the same thing in the active mode, do so.

Passive Voice Usage

The passive voice can be used by you. Both active voice and passive voice have advantages. The active voice reduces wordiness and makes your writing strong and interesting. The passive voice is more formal and more readily accepted in scientific writing because you can write without using personal pronouns or names of specific researchers. It represents the conventional means of impersonal reporting and gives the article an air of objectivity (Example: "Experiments have been conducted to test the hypothesis."). The passive voice also can be used to good effect in these ways:

1. To de-emphasize responsibility

   Example: Rather than "You made an error," write "An error was made."

2. To de-emphasize the writer

   Example: Instead of "I recommend," write "It is recommended that."

3. When the performer of the action is unknown or irrelevant

   Example: "A house was broken into on Main Street."

   Example: "Office mail is delivered twice a day."

Situations requiring use of passive voice occur infrequently. If your writing does not require these special situations, then reduce the unnecessary passive voice sentences that usually make your writing tedious and hard to understand. Remember, a sequence of passive verbs can have the air of authority, but what it often has is air!

How do you know if you've used too many passive constructions? On your document, circle (or make note of) every form of the verb *be* (*am, is, are, had, has, was, were, been*, etc.). *Passive*

> Pick up any *Scientific American* magazine and read the feature articles. You will notice very little passive voice writing in them because the magazine editors and the writers want the readers to read the articles.
>
> *(Continued)*

(Continued)

Therefore, they communicate with their readers in a concise and direct way without sacrificing objectivity. You should do the same when you are writing a scientific paper. Do not confuse objective with detached and wordy.

—Jeffrey Strausser,
Painless Writing (2001, p. 77)

voice constructions always include some form of "to be." If your page is covered with circles, rewrite the page using active verbs.

Tip 6: Use Transitional Words and Phrases

Transitions build bridges between your ideas and help you achieve a coherent document. They act as road signs that guide your readers from one idea to the next. Transitions help make your discussion easy to follow. Readers must understand how the topics relate to one another. Every sentence should be a logical sequel to the one that preceded it. You signal the relationships between sentences and paragraphs by the following sampling of transitional words and phrases:

Frequently Used Transitions

To Signal	Examples
Contrast	but, whereas, yet, still, however, nevertheless, despite, on the contrary, although, on the other hand, conversely
Addition	furthermore, subsequently, besides, next, moreover, also, similarly, too, second
Example	for instance, an illustration, thus, such as, that is, specifically
Time or place	afterwards, earlier, at the same time, subsequently, later, simultaneously, above, below, further on, so far, until now
Conclusion	therefore, in short, thus, then, in other words, in conclusion, consequently, as a result, accordingly, finally
Sequence	then, first, second, third, next

Tip 7: Simplify Your Vocabulary

Academic writers tend to use technical terms with abandon. They assume readers understand their specialized language. *Resist jargon— it excludes and mystifies.* If you must use a special term, explain it at the outset. Also remember to choose short words over long ones, especially if they have the same meaning. "Of the 701 words in Lincoln's Second Inaugural Address, a marvel of economy itself, 505 are words of one syllable and 122 are words of two syllables" (Zinsser, 1994, p. 112).

> Beware, then, of the long word that's no better than the short word: *assistance* (help), *numerous* (many), *facilitate* (ease), *individual* (man or woman), *remainder* (rest), *initial* (first), *implement* (do), *sufficient* (enough), *attempt* (try), *referred to as* (called), and hundreds more. (Zinsser, 1994, p. 16)

Tip 8: Use Quotations Sparingly

> The secret of good writing is to strip every sentence to its cleanest components. Every word that serves no function, every long word that could be a short word, every adverb that carries the same meaning that's already in the verb, every passive construction that leaves the reader unsure of who is doing what—these are the thousand and one adulterants that weaken the strength of a sentence. And they usually occur in proportion to education and rank.
>
> —William Zinsser, *On Writing Well* (1994, p. 7)

A research paper involves assimilating the works of others and giving proper acknowledgment. Over-quoting is a common mistake. Students often string together a series of quotations connected by words such as *similarly, likewise,* and *on the other hand.* Don't do this! Quotations should be used sparingly. Booth, Colomb, and Williams (1995) provided pertinent rules of thumb about when to use direct quotations and when to paraphrase your sources:

Use direct quotations:

- When you use the work of others as primary data
- When you want to appeal to their authority
- When the specific words of your source matter because

  o Those words have been important to other researchers
  o You want to focus on how your source says things
  o The words of the source are especially vivid or significant
  o You dispute your source and you want to state his or her case fairly

Paraphrase your sources:

- When you are more interested in content, findings, or claims than in how a source expresses himself or herself
- When you could have said the same thing yourself more clearly (p. 174)

It is important that you take control of interpreting the work of others. Excessive quoting is a form of laziness on your part. In doing so, you abdicate responsibility for being selective and doing your own interpretation for the reader.

Don't start your sentences with a quotation followed by your own words. Instead, start with your words and support them with quoted or paraphrased material.

Useful Verbs

A variety of useful words can introduce quotations and help avoid repetitive constructions such as "Smith said," or "Smith stated." More than just variety, these words also provide exactness.

acknowledged	confirmed	implied
addressed	contended	maintained
affirmed	contradicted	negated
agreed	declared	noted
argued	discussed	refuted
asserted	disputed	reported
believed	emphasized	thought
commented	endorsed	wrote

Further Reading

Bolker, J. (1998). *Writing your dissertation in fifteen minutes a day*. New York: Holt.
Danziger, E. (2001). *Get to the point*. New York: Three Rivers.
Hacker, D. (2007). *A writer's reference* (6th ed.). Boston: Bedford/St. Martin's.
O'Conner, P. (2009). *Woe is I: The grammarphobe's guide to better English in plain English* (3rd ed.). New York: Riverhead.
Shulman, M. (2005). *In focus: Strategies for academic writers*. Ann Arbor: University of Michigan Press.
Venolia, J. (2001). *Write right! A desktop digest of punctuation, grammar, and style*. Berkeley, CA: Ten Speed Press.

Helpful Websites

Purdue's Online Writing Lab (OWL)
- http://owl.english.purdue.edu/index.htm

The Writing Center (University of North Carolina)
- www.unc.edu/depts/wcweb

Duke University Research Guide
- http://library.duke.edu/services/instruction/libraryguide

Fussy Professor Starbuck's Cookbook of Handy-Dandy Prescriptions for Ambitious Academic Authors or Why I Hate Passive Verbs and Love My Word Processor

- http://pages.stern.nyu.edu/~wstarbuc/Writing/Fussy.htm

Summary

Scholarly, academic writing requires the ability to express your ideas logically, clearly, concisely, and with precision. Such writing requires command of basic writing skills such as logical organization, good sentence and paragraph construction, and appropriate transitions. This chapter offered eight tips designed to overcome basic problems dissertation students face in scholarly writing. The next chapter explains the components of a dissertation's introductory chapter and offers examples to clarify how to write each section.

PART IV

Climbing to Base Camp

Success is never the result of spontaneous combustion. You must set yourself on fire.

—Arnold Glasow

11

Writing the Introduction

The introduction chapter of your dissertation sets the stage for your study and typically consists of the following sections: the research problem, the theoretical or conceptual framework, purpose statement, research questions/hypotheses, significance of the study, delimitations, assumptions, definition of terms, organization of the remaining chapters, and a summary that states the key points made in the chapter. Most introductions in the social sciences follow a similar pattern; however, they may vary according to the type of research methodology used.

Usually, the overall structure of Chapter 1 moves from the general to the specific, beginning with an overview of the general area under study and ending with specific research questions/hypotheses. Think of writing Chapter 1 in a *V* or funnel-shaped fashion, as shown in Figure 11.1.

Let me elaborate on this funnel notion by guiding you through a thinking process to focus your introduction. First, draw a large funnel and fill it in to help you visually focus your topic. The top of the funnel begins with a description of the general area to be studied. Next, identify a *more specific* problem within the general area. Say why this problem is important to study and specify what is already known about the problem. Then, specify what is *not known* about the problem that is important to study. Finally, state a specific purpose statement in one or two sentences followed by research questions that guide the study.

Figure 11.1   Funnel from the General to the Specific

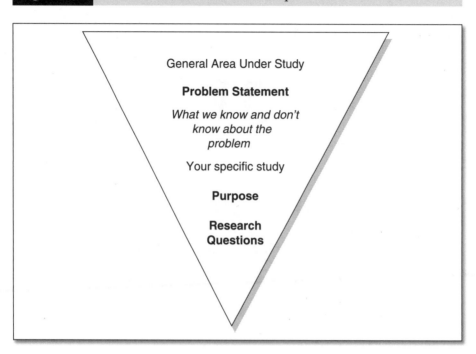

General Area Under Study

Problem Statement

*What we know and don't
know about the
problem*

Your specific study

Purpose

**Research
Questions**

Problem Statement

A research problem can be defined as "the issue that exists in the literature, in theory, or in practice that leads to a need for the study. The
research problem in a study becomes clear when the researcher asks,
'What is the need for this study?' or 'What problem influenced the need
to undertake this study?'" (Creswell, 2002, p. 80). Basically, the problem
statement provides an overview of the study. It states (1) what the study
is about, (2) why it is important and timely, (3) what contributions are
made to knowledge and practice, and (4) how the study fits into the
existing state of the art. The problem statement tells the story behind
the variables or concepts to be studied and provides background for the
purpose statement and research questions.

*answer
these
questions*

Figure 11.2   Example of Using a Funnel to Develop and Narrow the
Problem Statement

Improved student performance K–university continues to be a national priority

The availability of qualified teachers is critical to solving this problem

Past studies have shown a number of reasons for the teacher shortage: pay,
working conditions, support, recognition, and reward

There is also a shortage of qualified and available substitute teachers

Past studies indicate various reasons for the shortage of substitutes: pay, working conditions, support, recognition, reward, and student behavior

What isn't known is whether the decisions of current substitutes to stay in or leave teaching are the same as those in past studies

The purpose of this study is . . .

SOURCE: Gonzales (2002).

The problem statement should do the following:

- Have a *line of logic* that leads the reader to the purpose statement
- Provide a *background* to the variables or concepts to be studied
- Cite *literature sources,* but not extensively
- Conclude with the *"need to know"*

Line of Logic

The problem statement begins with a general introduction to the study and, through a careful line of reasoning, focuses down to become more detailed and specific to your study. Your writing should be clear, precise, and directional. There should be a sequential line of logic. "The delineation of the problem leads directly to the statement of the purpose. The purpose of any study is to help solve the stated problem" (Martin, 1980, p. 40). *An important point to remember is that the line of logic comes from you. It cannot be found directly in the literature.*

Background to the Study

Providing background information to the study requires answering the following questions:

1. What do we already know about this topic?
2. What do we *not* know about this topic? What has not been answered adequately in previous research and practice?
3. What do we want to know about this topic?

The problem statement is the discrepancy between what we already know and what we want to know. It is necessary to provide background information about both what is known and what is not known. The problem statement also tells the story about why we care—why we should conduct this study. It is important for the reader to know what is unique and different from previous research. Try to conceive of your study as a large jigsaw puzzle with a piece missing. Or you may conceive of your study as fulfilling an indicated need for further advancement of previous research. That missing piece is the gap you want to fill. To discover that missing piece, you must read widely in the literature base of your topic area.

When all of these studies are aggregated, you can then tell something about the problem's domain. (See Figure 11.3.)

Figure 11.3 Defining the Problem's Domain

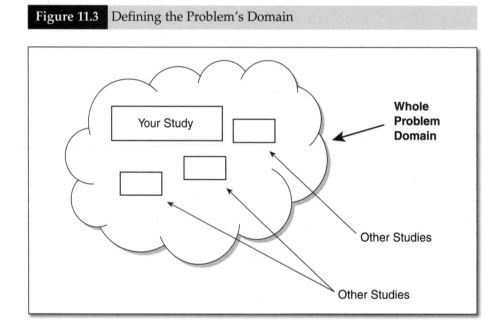

Literature Sources

The variables or factors you selected for study must exist within some conceptual or theoretical framework that you develop from reading the literature. You cannot just pull your topic out of a hat. Appropriate citations from the literature help provide a justification for selecting these variables or concepts. Creating a conceptual framework is one of the few places where you have the opportunity to display original thought. If, however, you conduct an inductive qualitative study, your variables or concepts emerge from the data. Rather than starting with a conceptual framework, you investigate broad, general areas that become more focused through data gathering in the field.

Your problem statement must explain how your study fits into the existing state of the art. Martin (1980), in his book *Writing and Defending a Thesis or Dissertation in Psychology and Education,* delineated some of the circumstances into which your problem might fit:

1. There is little or no research on a particular topic.

2. There is some research but it has not been applied to enough samples or in enough situations to be considered a reliable phenomenon.

3. There is a good deal of research, but the findings are contradictory. (pp. 39–40)

Citing the literature helps you build a case for why your research should be undertaken. The references and quotations support your arguments. However, keep in mind that in most cases, citations should be used sparingly in the problem statement. It is not a formal review of the literature.

For impact, keep your sentences short and write an opening sentence that stimulates interest. In short, your introductory chapter should convince your readers of the study's need and value.

Need to Know

What is the need for this particular study? Why does this specific study need to be conducted? So what? What will your study add to the knowledge base? "The need for the study is established by showing that there is a problem of some importance, establishing that there is a gap in the knowledge base, and by showing why filling that particular gap is important or at least relevant" (Ogden, 1993, p. 84). However, the major discussion of the study's importance may be found in the section "Significance of the Study."

Common Errors in Writing the Problem Statement

Here are some common errors students make in submitting drafts of their problem statements.

- Failing to get to the point. Avoid tedious length in introducing the study. The reader wants to know what your study is about.
- Making the reader believe that we already know the answer. If we know it, then we don't need to study it.
- Covering extraneous issues, whether interesting or not. These are "rabbit runs"—interesting but irrelevant to the topic. Resist the temptation to share with the reader the volume of interesting but irrelevant information you accumulated.
- Being inconsistent. The problem should be clearly and logically related to the purpose statement and research questions.

- Stating what we should *do* rather than what we want to *know.* Such phrases as "we must . . . ," "we should . . . ," and "it is imperative that . . ." belong in a position paper. In short, stay off a soapbox.
- Writing in "dissertationese" rather than in English. This causes your writing to be stilted, awkward, and artificial. Just say what you mean in natural phrases.
- Using unnecessary technical language and jargon. This keeps the reader from understanding the main idea of what you're trying to say.
- Using extensive quotations and references. These get in the way of the logical flow of ideas.
- Using abstruse arguments. Refrain from making points that are unclear or difficult to understand. Write in a clear, simple, and straightforward manner.
- Engaging in personal reflections or editorializing. Reserve this for Chapter 5.
- Making unsupported claims or statements. The problem must be written in the context of theory and relevant literature.
- Using disjointed recitation of the studies cited. *You* create the line of logic and use literature citations to substantiate *your* points.

The opening sentences of your dissertation should be approached thoughtfully and carefully, for this is the place to win or lose your audience. Therefore, introduce your topic in a way that engages readers— that captures their interest and makes them want to continue reading. Creswell (2008) called these opening lines the "narrative hook," a term he claimed is "drawn from English composition, meaning words that serve to draw, engage, or hook the reader into the study" (p. 102). A convincing narrative hook, according to Creswell (2005), could include the following:

1. Statistical data (e.g., "More than 50 percent of the adult population experiences depression today.")

2. A provocative question (e.g., "Why are school policies that ban smoking in high schools not being enforced?")

3. A clear need for research (e.g., "School suspension is drawing increased attention among scholars in teacher education.") (p. 67)

There are a variety of other possibilities for introducing your study; the main thing to remember is to begin in an engaging manner that will interest your audience so they keep on reading.

Theoretical or Conceptual Framework

Doctoral students hate to hear these words from their dissertation advisor: "Your study sounds promising, but what is your theoretical framework?" This question is often met with silence, raised eyebrows, or shrugged shoulders indicating more information is needed about this term. In discussing the theoretical framework, Merriam (2001) stated, "A colleague of mine once commented that if she could have figured out what a theoretical framework was early on, she could have cut a year off of her graduate studies! Indeed, the theoretical or conceptual framework of a study and where theory fits into a research study continue to mystify and frustrate many a novice (and sometimes experienced) researcher" (pp. 44–45). Few texts or books about writing a dissertation or thesis discuss the process, importance, or purpose of developing a conceptual or theoretical framework and making it explicit. It is often the missing link in student scholarship. Hopefully, this section will ground your understanding in this important aspect of designing and clarifying your research.

What Is a Conceptual or Theoretical Framework?

It is a lens through which your research problem is viewed. It can be a theory, a construct that conceptualizes your study's focus, or a research perspective. Miles and Huberman (1994) defined it this way: "A conceptual framework explains, either graphically or in narrative form, the main things to be studied—the key factors, constructs, or variables—and the presumed relationships among them. Frameworks can be rudimentary or elaborate, theory-driven or commonsensical, descriptive, or causal" (p. 18). Some of the visual forms a conceptual framework might take could be tree diagrams, mind maps, flow charts, concept maps, or diagrams such as triangles, circles, and so on. In their book, *Qualitative Data Analysis,* Miles and Huberman (1994) provided several graphic illustrations followed by descriptive narrative that served as examples of conceptual or theoretical frameworks.

The conceptual or theoretical framework provides the boundaries, or scaffolding, for your study. Like a microscope, it narrows your field of vision, thus helping you limit the scope of your study. After all, it is usually not possible to study everything about your research topic. A conceptual or theoretical framework identifies which of the "key factors, constructs, or variables" (Miles & Huberman, 1994, p. 18) are in and which are out. Making your conceptual or theoretical framework explicit provides clarity for the reader as to exactly what your study is about and provides the focus and content for making decisions about your study's design. By not grounding your study within an explicit conceptual or theoretical frame, your study takes on a "so what?" quality.

How Does a Conceptual Framework Differ From a Theoretical Framework?

Often, the terms *conceptual framework* and *theoretical framework* are used interchangeably, and rarely is a differentiation made. A theory is a discussion about related concepts, assumptions, and generalizations, while concepts can be defined as words or phrases that represent several interrelated ideas. If your study is grounded in a particular theory or theories, then perhaps the better term would be *theoretical framework*, since theory would be used to explain the particular phenomenon under study. It implies a higher level of conceptual organization. If your study does not include a specific theory, it still contains concepts and subconcepts that define the interrelationship of the ideas contained in your study. Some studies contain a review of theory as well as a conceptual framework. I recommend a conference with your dissertation advisor to determine the best approach for your particular study. Remember, no study is without some implicit framework. Your challenge is to discover it and make it explicit.

Why Do You Need a Conceptual or Theoretical Framework?

A well-defined conceptual or theoretical framework helps you to view your area of interest more acutely. Like a telescope or microscope, a conceptual or theoretical framework narrows and brings into focus your field of vision, which is necessary for limiting the scope of your study. It helps define the research problem and structures the writing of your literature review. In addition, it acts as a filtering tool to select appropriate research questions and to guide data collection, analysis, and interpretation of findings. According to Merriam (2001), "All aspects of the study are affected by its theoretical framework" (p. 47).

How Do You Find a Conceptual or Theoretical Framework?

The best way to select an appropriate conceptual or theoretical framework for your study is to immerse yourself in the research and theoretical literature related to your topic of interest. You may not find a specific theory to guide your study; however, you will discover a variety of interrelated core concepts and subconcepts from which to frame your study.

EXAMPLE 1 OF A CONCEPTUAL FRAMEWORK

Following are sections from a quantitative dissertation about student persistence and academic success in an institution of higher education. The researcher prepared a separate section in Chapter One devoted to the study's underlying theories.

CONCEPTUAL FRAMEWORK

To properly frame this study...it was appropriate to go to the recognized experts in college persistence. These theorists studied college persistence for over 35 years and developed models that have been tested and validated.

Student persistence is complex, made up of many variables (Lewallen, 1993). Studies since the 1970s attempted to isolate the most important and influential elements of student retention, attrition, and ultimately persistence to bachelor degree completion. Two theorists who heavily influenced the direction of this research were Vincent Tinto and Alexander Astin (Blecher, Michael, & Hagedon, 2002; Colbert, 1999; Hutto, 2002).

Vincent Tinto in 1975 developed his "Model of Student Departure," which postulated that students come to a college with a particular background molded by their own unique genetics and environmental experiences and are guided by certain aspirations toward particular goal completions. This background and goal setting impacted the academic and social integration of the student at the university. Ultimately, Tinto theorized that the successful academic and social integration of a student led to successful persistence to degree completion (Blecher, Michael, & Hagedorn, 2002; Tinto, 1975). Tinto's theory has been widely quoted and reviewed over the last 30 years as evidenced by over 400 citations and at least 170 dissertations focusing on this theory (Braxton, Milem, & Sullivan, 2000). The basic precepts of the theory have been affirmed by many researchers (Aitken, 1982; Benjamin, 1993; Pascarella, 1983; Terenzini, 1980, 1977, 1985).

In 1970, Alexander Astin began with a general education model focusing on how students are impacted by their college experience. He then developed and expanded it over the next few years and referred to it as the "Input-Environment-Output" persistence model (Astin, 1970, 1975). Students enter higher education with unique "input" variables, again based on their own genetics and particular environmental experiences (Astin, 1970). Astin described these inputs as...Astin defined the "environment" variables as "those aspects of higher educational institutions that are capable of affecting the student" (Astin, 1970, p. 3). These environmental variables can be anything from institutional policies, associations with other students, support programs, facilities, to specific curriculum (Astin, 1970).

(Continued)

(Continued)

The final aspect of the model, the "output" variables, refers to...In conjunction with this structure, Astin designed a "Theory of Involvement" and theorized that the level of involvement of a student's interactions within the university environment was a major factor in the eventual persistence of the student (Astin, 1970, 1984).

...Hutto's literature review on student retention revealed that Astin is considered the foremost researcher on student involvement theory primarily because...Astin has led the nation's longest running study of college environments (Astin, 2003).

Both Tinto and Astin use an Input-Environment-Output approach to student persistence. Both acknowledge the role of student biological and environmental independent variables on the dependent outcome variables of persistence and ultimate academic success and the possible mediating role of university environmental variables on the input variables.

Note: The researcher then proceeded to describe the applicability of the Input-Environment-Output Model to his particular study.

Spindle, B. (2006). *A study of Alaska native student persistence and academic success at the University of Alaska Anchorage.* Doctoral Dissertation, University of La Verne.

EXAMPLE 2 OF A CONCEPTUAL FRAMEWORK

This example is from a dissertation titled "An Exploratory Study of the Ways in Which Superintendents Use Their Emotional Intelligence to Address Conflict in Their Organizations" by Lori Geery (1997). Her purpose was the following:

> The purpose of this study was to describe the knowledge, skills, behaviors, and strategies associated with emotional intelligence that superintendents perceived they use to address conflict in their organizations. This study also determined the impact use of emotional intelligence had on superintendents' perceptions of their ability to lead and manage their organizations. (Geery, 1997)

The conceptual framework for this study was the five concept areas of emotional intelligence: understanding their own emotions, managing their own emotions, motivating themselves, recognizing emotions of others, and handling relationships with others. The matrix that outlines this conceptual framework follows. Notice how this framework mirrors the purpose of the study.

	Knowledge	Skills	Behaviors	Strategies
Understanding their own emotions	-Uses emotional self-awareness -Uses emotional self-knowledge	-Displays self-regard -Is intuitive -Is insightful -Is reflective	-Is confident -Is assertive	-Recognizes one's strengths and weaknesses -Capitalizes on strengths and improves weaknesses through self-improvement
Managing their own emotions	-Understands and uses impulse control -Understands and uses self-control	-Is resilient -Is flexible -Displays a tolerance for dealing with stress	-Holds back negative emotions to remain positive -Displays positive emotional behavior	-Reframes problems -Uses humor -Takes time out to relax
Motivating themselves	-Understands and believes in one's potential (potency)	-Is optimistic -Is hopeful -Is persistent -Approaches challenges with enthusiasm	-Delays gratification -Displays positive energy -Accepts responsibility for own behavior -Focuses attention on the task at hand	-Sets personal goals -Breaks down large tasks into smaller steps and -Celebrates small successes
Recognizing emotions of others	-Understands and demonstrates empathy	-Reads people's nonverbal behavior -Listens actively -Demonstrates insight about other's feelings, motives, and concerns	-Pays attention to people and relationships -Mirrors other's movements and tones -Demonstrates regard and compassion for others	-Develops rapport with colleagues and employees -Allows employees to express emotions -Provides emotional support for others
Handling relationships with others	-Understands how to develop relationships	-Influences, persuades, and inspires others -Appropriate expression and transfer of emotion -Harnesses the willing participation of others	-Demonstrates respect for others -Recognizes and responds appropriately to people's feelings and concerns -Makes personal connections with others -Promotes cooperation	-Models emotional intelligence -Builds trust in relationships -Boosts organizational morale -Builds collaboration among people -Gives praise, recognition, and rewards

Conceptual Framework That Is Used to Describe and Classify Emotional Intelligence (Geery, 1997, p. 100).

To see additional examples of describing a conceptual or theoretical framework, refer to John Creswell's book, *Research Design: Qualitative, Quantitative, and Mixed Methods Approaches* (2nd ed.). In this book, Creswell (2002) provided models for writing a quantitative theoretical perspective section (see pp. 127–130). He also provided a description and examples of qualitative theory use (see pp. 131–136).

Purpose Statement

By the time the reader gets to the purpose statement, there should be no doubt about what you will be doing in your study. The purpose statement, usually written in a single sentence or paragraph, clearly and succinctly states the intent of your study—what exactly you're going to find out. It represents the essence of your study and reflects its parameters. The purpose statement, according to Creswell (2009), "is the most important statement in the entire study, and it needs to be clearly and specifically presented" (p. 111). The purpose is clarified when you specify the variables or concepts under study and indicate whether your study is descriptive in nature or whether it is a relationship or differences study. In any one study, you may find one or more of these three types of measurements. Following are some examples to help you differentiate among them:

Example 1: A Purpose Statement in a Descriptive Study

The purpose of this study was to determine which strategies principals used to implement shared decision making in selected elementary schools and to determine how effective they were perceived to be by the principal, a teacher, and a parent at each site. (Walkington, 1991)

Example 2: A Purpose Statement in a Relationships Study

The purpose of this study was to identify the relationship between the perceived effectiveness of teacher work teams and teacher motivational needs.

Example 3: A Purpose Statement in a Differences Study

The purpose of this study was to determine whether there is a significant difference between the limited-English-speaking high school students attending year-round schools and limited-English-proficient students attending traditional high schools in the areas of (1) student attendance, (2) student grade point average, (3) student academic achievement as measured by units earned toward graduation, and (4) student oral English-language acquisition as measured by Language Assessment Survey (LAS). (Miranda, 1993)

Example 4: A Purpose Statement in a Differences and Relationships Study

The purpose of this study was to determine the differences between public and non-public school special education principals and teachers of students with severe emotional disturbances on their leadership orientations. It also determined whether a relationship existed between these leadership orientations and variables of school success as measured by student absenteeism, suspensions, expulsions, and teacher absenteeism. (Hernandez, 1996)

Example 5: A Purpose Statement in a Descriptive and Differences Study

The purpose of this study was to describe the collective bargaining procedures used by selected community college districts and the climates of the colleges. It was also the purpose of this study to describe the differences between a population with training in non-adversarial collective bargaining strategies and a population without training in collective bargaining strategies. (Garcia-Lipscomb, 1997)

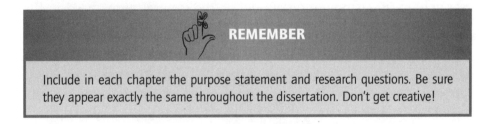

REMEMBER

Include in each chapter the purpose statement and research questions. Be sure they appear exactly the same throughout the dissertation. Don't get creative!

It is important to realize that purpose statements vary according to specialized research designs. A qualitative purpose statement uses words drawn from that specialized line of inquiry and often reflects the procedures of an emerging design format. Sometimes qualitative researchers use words such as *intent, aim,* or *objective* to draw attention to the study's intent. Examples that illustrate the difference between qualitative, quantitative, and mixed-methods purpose statements can be found in *Research Design: Qualitative, Quantitative, and Mixed Methods Approaches* by Creswell (2009).

Research Questions/Hypotheses

"A question well stated is a question half answered."

Your topic was introduced, background information provided, and the purpose clearly stated. In this section of the dissertation, you state the research questions or hypotheses for the study. Your research questions/ hypotheses guide the study and usually provide the structure for presenting the results of the research. Generally, good research questions should have the following:

- Clear variables/concepts
- Obvious measurement type (description, relationship, difference)
- No *how* or *why* questions
- "Thing words" clarified (success, processes, achievement, factors, etc.)
- No questions that can be answered by counting or by answering "yes" or "no"

In quantitative studies, research hypotheses state the expectations of the researcher concerning the relationship between variables. They indicate what the researcher thinks the outcome of the study will be. If your study is looking at differences, you may wish to state your hypotheses as null hypotheses that state there is no difference between variables. Following is an example of a descriptive purpose statement with research questions. Notice the alignment between them. The research questions operationally define the general terms used in the purpose statement (e.g., *changes* and *factors*).

EXAMPLE

Purpose Statement

The purposes of this study were to describe the changes that occurred at three California middle schools where school-linked services were delivered and to identify the factors that facilitated and barriers that impeded the delivery of services.

RESEARCH QUESTIONS

1. What services were delivered at California middle schools, and how did students access these services?

2. What changes occurred in the resources of money, personnel, facilities, time, and energy?

3. What changes occurred in the roles and responsibilities of school personnel?

4. What changes in curricular or extracurricular areas occurred since the delivery of school-linked services?

5. What changes in student discipline or parent involvement occurred since the delivery of school-linked services?

6. What factors at the school sites facilitated the delivery of school-linked services?

7. What barriers impeded the delivery of school-linked services?

SOURCE: Kinley (1996).

Because the qualitative research paradigm is characterized by the emergence of questions during the course of data collection and analysis, the author may (a) present the original research questions in this chapter and then, in the methodology chapter, discuss how these changed during data collection and analysis; or (b) present the final questions that emerged during data collection and analysis.

Significance of the Study

This section is a more detailed explanation of the *why* of your study. Does it explore an important issue, meet a recognized need, or fill in a gap in the knowledge base? You must build an argument for the worth or significance of your research—how it should be useful to knowledge, practitioners, and policy makers.

You have to convince your reader, especially your advisor and committee, of the need for this particular study. To support your argument, you can summarize writings of experts who identified your problem as an important one and urged that research be conducted about it. Second, you can show specific data that indicate the severity of the problem and the need to resolve it.

Ogden (1993) provided some important points to remember about writing this section. First, she stated, "The rationale should be understandable to any reasonably educated individual, not just to people in your field." Second, she cautioned you not to "oversell the contribution to the field." It will not necessarily solve a national problem. Finally, she pointed out that "no matter which way the results come out, the value of this study could be defended" (Ogden, 1993, p. 86).

Creswell (2009) provided additional insight into writing the significance section of your dissertation. In designing this section, he advises including the following:

- Three or four reasons that the study adds to the scholarly research and literature in the field
- Three or four reasons about how the study helps improve practice
- Three or four reasons as to why the study will improve policy (p. 107)

Delimitations

This section clarifies the boundaries of your study. It is the way to indicate to the reader how you narrowed your study's scope. You control the delimitations—what will be included and what will be left out. Following are some typical delimitations:

- Time of the study: February 2008 through April 2009
- Location of the study: districts in southern California or urban areas only
- Sample of the study: principals and superintendents
- Selected aspects of the problem
- Selected criteria of the study

Following are some ways to express a dissertation's delimitations:

1. Only those districts with student enrollments less than 1,000 were included in this study.

2. Those surveyed in this study consisted of female managers in their first supervisory position.

3. The study included only those organizations that matched the selection criteria established for the study. The criteria for selection included . . . .

Often the terms *delimitation* and *limitation* are confused. Mauch and Birch (1993) offered a clear distinction between the two. They stated,

"A limitation is a factor that may or will affect the study in an important way, but *is not under control* of the researcher; a delimitation differs, principally, in that it *is controlled* by the researcher" (p. 103). Since limitations primarily involve the inherent weaknesses in the methodology, they are usually placed in the methodology section.

Assumptions

Not all studies include assumptions. Whether or not they are indicated depends on the desires of your advisor and committee members. Basically, assumptions are what you take for granted relative to your study. Following are some examples of assumptions:

1. The sample studied was representative of the total population of nurses employed at the St. Paul's Memorial Hospital.

2. Responses received from the participating managers accurately reflected their professional opinions.

3. High school students can remember what their perceptions were of the bilingual program in which they participated 10 to 12 years ago.

4. The participants in this study answered all of the interview questions openly and honestly.

Definition of Terms

This section of the dissertation provides the definition for the terms used that do not have a commonly known meaning or that have the possibility of being misunderstood. These terms should be operationally defined—that is, defined according to how the terms are used in your study. You can choose to define them in any way you like in order to clarify what you mean when you use that particular term. Unless they are clearly defined, they can be open to numerous interpretations. For example, the term *achievement* in education can refer to a variety of meanings. One operational definition may be the level of test scores throughout a school, or it could mean skill in playing the piano. It is appropriate to paraphrase or to specifically cite definitions used from the literature. Following are some examples of definition of terms used in dissertations:

Transformational leader. Someone in authority who articulates a clear vision for the future.

Empowerment. A process that enables people to do what they do best and for which they are held accountable.

Site-based management. A system that increases people's authority at the school site and involves them in implementing decisions.

REMEMBER

Define each new term the first time it appears in the study.

Organization of the Study

Usually, Chapter 1 concludes with a section that delineates the contents of the remaining chapters in the study. Here is an example:

> The remainder of the study is organized into five chapters, a bibliography, and appendixes in the following manner. Chapter 2 presents a review of the related literature dealing with evolving trends in the practices and procedures used to evaluate superintendents. Chapter 3 delineates the research design and methodology of the study. The instrument used to gather the data, the procedures followed, and determination of the sample selected for study are described. An analysis of the data and a discussion of the findings are presented in Chapter 4. Chapter 5 contains the summary, conclusions, and recommendations of the study. The study concludes with a bibliography and appendixes.

Summary

When writing your dissertation's introductory chapter, be sure to include background information to all the variables and concepts directly related to your study, the importance of your study to the field, and an explicit discussion of your study's conceptual or theoretical framework. Write a clear and succinct purpose statement and research questions that clearly define the parameters of your study. It is also important to include a delimitations section that clarifies the scope of your study and a definition of terms section that operationally defines the specific terms used in your study. A concluding statement delineates the contents of the study's remaining chapters.

The next chapter guides you through the process of selecting and describing your study's methodology.

12

Selecting and Describing the Methodology

Selecting the Methodology

Beginning the climb on the dissertation mountain involves choosing a dissertation topic, conducting a review of the literature, and selecting and describing a research methodology. These are not linear processes; they undulate back and forth and often go on simultaneously. Reviewing the literature grounds you in understanding what is known and not known about your study's topic and helps provide the basis for selecting an appropriate methodology. Whatever methodology you choose, you need to understand the techniques and processes of that particular method. Very few students remember well the content from their research methodology or statistics courses.

Selection Considerations

Students frequently ask, "How do I go about selecting a methodology for my study?" The answer isn't simple; it is possible to identify several different methodological approaches for a single topic. Methodology selection rests primarily on the (1) problem to be investigated, (2) purpose of the study, (3) theory base, and (4) nature of the data. Selection may also depend on your research skills and those of your committee members. I recommend that one of your committee members possess the expertise in the methodology you select. How comfortable are you with statistics? Do you have the required literary writing skills necessary for qualitative research? It is essential that you are able to express yourself *clearly* and *explicitly.* Don't worry if you do not feel comfortable with your level of knowledge about research methodology or with the skills required to conduct an original research study. In my experience, most students do not come to the dissertation process confident and eager to apply research skills. "Learning by doing" is the name of the game. With guidance from your committee, your learning evolves over time as you proceed through each stage of the dissertation. *Don't try to make your study fit a predetermined research methodology.*

The research approach you select for your study will be quantitative, qualitative, or a combination of the two. In this section, I present a comparison of these two paradigms but focus on the qualitative approach because of the increased interest and use of this methodology in education and the social sciences. This book, however, is not a methodology text, and I refer you to the Further Reading section at the end of this chapter for detailed information in the various methodological approaches.

The Methodology of Research

All research methodology can be classified under two broad generic categories: *quantitative* or *qualitative.* Each has a variety of submethodologies, or designs, with their own protocol for collecting and analyzing data. A hybrid approach is obtained when quantitative and qualitative approaches are used together. Blending these two approaches generally allows greater depth of understanding and insight than what is possible using just one approach. Plus, blending helps overcome the biases inherent in each method.

Quantitative Versus Qualitative Research

What is the difference between qualitative and quantitative research? Staindack and Staindack (1988) explained it this way: "Qualitative research differs from quantitative research in its theoretical/philosophical rationale" (p. 4). In philosophical terms, the quantitative approach is called *logical positivism.* Inquiry begins with a specific plan—a set of detailed questions or hypotheses. Researchers seek facts and causes of human behavior and want to know a lot about a few variables so differences can be identified. They collect data that are primarily numerical and result from surveys, tests, experiments, and so on. Most quantitative approaches manipulate variables and control the research setting. Quantitative designs include descriptive research, experimental research, quasi-experimental research, ex post facto/causal comparative research, and correlational research.

> Not everything that can be counted counts, and not everything that counts can be counted.
>
> —Albert Einstein

The qualitative approach is based on the philosophical orientation called *phenomenology*, which focuses on people's experience from their perspective. Inquiry begins with broad, general questions about the area under investigation. Researchers seek a holistic picture—a comprehensive and complete understanding of the phenomena they are studying. They go into the field to collect data. They may make observations; conduct in-depth, open-ended interviews; or look at written documents. Rather than numbers, the data are words that describe people's knowledge, opinions, perceptions, and feelings as well as detailed descriptions of people's actions, behaviors, activities, and interpersonal interactions. Qualitative research may also focus on organizational processes. In other words, qualitative researchers look at the essential character or nature of something, not the quantity (how much, how many). This approach is sometimes called naturalistic inquiry because the research is conducted in real-world settings; no attempt is made to manipulate the environment. Researchers are interested in the meanings people attach to the activities and events in their world and are open to whatever emerges. Qualitative research is really an umbrella term that refers to several research genres that share certain characteristics. They go by different names, such as case study research, historical research, ethnography, grounded theory, narrative analysis, action research, and hermeneutics.

Why Do Qualitative Research?

Strauss and Corbin (1990) offer five reasons for doing qualitative research:

1. The conviction of the researcher based on research experience

2. The nature of the research problem

3. To uncover and understand what lies behind any phenomenon about which little is yet known

4. To gain novel and fresh slants on things about which quite a bit is already known

5. To give intricate details of phenomena that are difficult to convey with quantitative methods (p. 19)

The most salient differences between qualitative and quantitative approaches are listed in Figure 12.1.

Figure 12.1	Research Methodologies: A Comparison

Qualitative	Quantitative
• Naturalistic designs • Descriptive • Inductive analysis (generate hypotheses) • Observations/interviews • The researcher is the instrument • Trustworthiness depends on the researcher's skill and competence • Depth (collection of intensive data) • Small samples (purposive sampling) • Discovering/exploring concepts • Extrapolations	• Experimental designs • Explanatory • Deductive analysis (test hypotheses) • Standardized measures • Validity depends on careful instrument construction • Breadth (limited set of variables measured) • Large samples (random sampling) • Testing/verifying theories and concepts • Generalizations

Both research orientations play an important role in extending knowledge. Whichever you select for your study, be sure to read widely in that methodological area so you are knowledgeable about the analysis and data collection procedures necessary to conduct your study. Remember, in the end, you must justify your choice of methodology and clarify why it was the best way to conduct your study. Because there are no inferential statistics to be performed in qualitative research, some students mistakenly believe it to be easier to conduct than a quantitative study. This is not true! Analyzing huge amounts of qualitative data into meaningful themes and patterns is an awesome task requiring considerable time and effort. According to Patton (2002), "On average, a one-hour interview will yield 10 to 15 single-spaced pages of text; 10 two-hour interviews will yield roughly 200 to 300 pages of transcripts" (p. 440).

Mixed Methods

Although qualitative and quantitative approaches are grounded in different paradigms, it is possible to combine them into one study. The mixed-methods approach is expanding as a viable methodology in the social and human sciences, evidenced by a variety of books and journals reporting and promoting mixed-methods research. Creswell (2002) reported that "entire books now exist about procedures for conducting mixed methods studies—similar books were not available a decade ago (Greene & Caracelli, 1997; Newman & Benz, 1998; Reichardt & Rallis, 1994; Tashakkori & Teddlie, 1998)" (p. 208).

Here are some ways to incorporate both qualitative and quantitative approaches into a single study. Numerical data may be included in a qualitative study, and narrative data (such as open-ended questionnaire responses) may be included in a quantitative study. For example, you may start gathering data with a survey to get a broad perspective and then select cases to study in depth by conducting open-ended interviews. You may also start with a case study design and find variables to ask on a survey. Strauss and Corbin (1990) offered other examples of how qualitative and quantitative approaches can be combined: "One might use qualitative data to illustrate or clarify quantitatively derived findings; or, one could quantify demographic findings. Or, use some form of quantitative data to partially validate one's qualitative analysis" (p. 19).

Qualitative and quantitative approaches in a single study complement each other by providing results with greater breadth and depth. Combining *what* with a possible *why* adds power and richness to your explanation of the data. With quantitative methods, you can summarize large amounts of data and reach generalizations based on statistical projections. Qualitative research tells a story from the viewpoint of the participants that provides rich descriptive detail. Figure 12.2 is an example of a table from a dissertation by Clark (2002) that combines qualitative and quantitative data.

| Figure 12.2 | Example: Summary of Responses From Interviews Describing Collaboration Activities |

Interview Question	Summary Phrase	Frequency
Describe how the partners worked together in building the school	Cooperative working relationship	9
	Consistent communication with partner	6
	Contentious negotiations	6
	Easier to work with high-level decision maker	1
	Outward appearance of good relationship with partner, but then there is reality	1

Gay and Airasian (2003) offered a practical resource for understanding how to mix qualitative and quantitative methods. They offered three models of mixed-methods research:

1. The QUAL-Quan model where qualitative data are collected first and are more heavily weighted than quantitative

2. The QUAN-Qual model where quantitative data are collected first and are more heavily weighted than qualitative

3. The QUAN-QUAL model where qualitative and quantitative are equally weighted and are collected concurrently (pp. 184–185)

Following are some resources that explain in detail various research designs within the qualitative, quantitative, and mixed-methods paradigms. Numerous books are available on research methodology, many highly theoretical—designed for professional researchers. I selected these books for their readability, clarity in explaining research concepts, and usefulness in writing dissertations.

Further Reading

Qualitative Research

Corbin, J., & Strauss, A. (2008). *Basics of qualitative research* (3rd ed.). Thousand Oaks, CA: Sage.

Denzin, N. K., & Lincoln, Y. S. (Eds.). (2005). *The Sage handbook of qualitative research* (3rd ed.). Thousand Oaks, CA: Sage.

Lightfoot, S. L. (1985). *The good high school: Portraits of character and culture.* New York: Basic Books. (An exemplary model for case study research)

Merriam, S. B. (2001). *Qualitative research and case study applications in education.* San Francisco: Jossey-Bass.

Miles, M. B., & Huberman, A. M. (1994). *Qualitative data analysis: An expanded sourcebook.* Thousand Oaks, CA: Sage.

Patton, M. Q. (2002). *Qualitative research & evaluation methods* (3rd ed.). Thousand Oaks, CA: Sage.

Rossman, G. B., & Rallis, S. F. (2003). *Learning in the field: An introduction to qualitative research* (2nd ed.). Thousand Oaks, CA: Sage.

Journals

- *Forum: Qualitative Social Research*
- *International Journal of Qualitative Methods*
- *The Qualitative Report*
- *Qualitative Research Journal*

Resources on the Web

Association for Qualitative Research

- www.aqr.org.au/

Forum : Qualitative Social Research

- http://qualitative-research.net/fqs

Qual Page : Resources for Qualitative Research

- www.qualitativeresearch.uga.edu/QualPage

Internet E-mail Discussion Groups (listservs)

QUAL-L Qualitative Research Mailing List

- www.scu.edu.au/schools/gcm/ar/arr/qual.html

QUALRS-L Qualitative Research for the Human Sciences

- http://www.lsoft.com/scripts/wl.exe?sl1=qualrs-l&h=listserv
.uga.edu

NOTE: These lists of resources are not exhaustive and may change over time.

Quantitative Research

Babbie, E. (2001). *Survey research methods* (9th ed.). Belmont, CA: Wadsworth.

Cox, J., & Cox, K. (2007). *Your opinion, please! How to build the best questionnaires in the field of education* (2nd ed.). Thousand Oaks, CA: Corwin.

Fowler, F. J. (2002). *Survey research methods* (3rd ed.). Thousand Oaks, CA: Sage.

Gravetter, F. J., & Wallnau, L. B. (2008). *Statistics for the behavioral sciences* (8th ed.). Belmont, CA: Wadsworth.

Marsh, C. (2009). *Exploring data: An introduction to data analysis for social scientists* (2nd ed.). New York: Polity.

Tufte, E. R. (2001). *The visual display of quantitative information* (2nd ed.). Cheshire, CT: Graphics Press.

Journals

Journal of Applied Quantitative Methods

- http://jaqm.ro

Journal of Statistics Education

- www.amstat.org/PUBLICATIONS/JSE

Resources on the Web

Rice Virtual Lab in Statistics

- http://onlinestatbook.com/rvls.html

Statistics.com

- www.statistics.com

Electronic Statistics Textbook

- www.statsoft.com/textbook/stathome.html

Mixed-Methods Research

Creswell, J. W. (2009). *Research design: Qualitative, quantitative, and mixed methods approaches* (3rd ed.). Thousand Oaks, CA: Sage.

Creswell, J. W., & Plano Clark, V. L. (2007). *Designing and conducting mixed methods research*. Thousand Oaks, CA: Sage.

Gay, L. R., Mills, G., & Peter, A. (2008). *Educational research: Competencies for analysis and applications* (9th ed.). Upper Saddle River, NJ: Merrill Prentice Hall.

Neuman, W. L. (2005). *Social research methods: Quantitative and qualitative approaches* (6th ed.). Boston: Allyn & Bacon.

Tashakkori, A., & Teddlie, C. (Eds.). (2003). *Handbook of mixed methods in the social and behavior sciences*. Thousand Oaks, CA: Sage.

Journals

Journal of Mixed Methods Research

* http://mmr.sagepub.com

Describing the Methodology

The methodology chapter of a dissertation describes the design and the specific procedures used in conducting your study. It is vital that this section is clear, comprehensive, and sufficiently detailed so that other researchers can adequately judge the results you obtain and can validly replicate the study. In a quantitative study, the methodology chapter usually contains the following sections: introduction, research design, population and sample, sampling procedures, instrumentation, data collection procedures, data analysis, and limitations. Qualitative studies typically use different terminology in describing the methodology section. For example, a qualitative study's sections often include the following: rationale and assumptions for the qualitative design, type of design, researcher's role, site selection, data sources, data collection techniques, managing and recording data, data analysis procedures, methods for verification or trustworthiness, and limitations. Following is a description of these sections.

Introduction

You may introduce the methodology chapter several ways, depending on the style and preference of your advisor and committee. Generally, there is an opening paragraph stating the chapter's organization. This is sometimes followed with a restatement of your study's purpose and research questions. A brief description of the problem might also be included.

Research Design

In this section, state the type of research and design used in the study as well as the rationale for your selection. The research design you select is based on the purpose and nature of your study. Some alternative designs are historical, descriptive, developmental, case study, correlational, ex post facto, true experimental, and quasi-experimental. Isaac and Michael (1995) provided an excellent resource to help you understand and describe the research design appropriate for your study. Following is an example from a dissertation of one way to describe a descriptive study's methodology:

EXAMPLE

Descriptive research methodology was used to identify the current socialization processes for beginning elementary principals in the central coast region of California. This method was selected because it is a means to describe systematically, factually, and accurately the characteristics of an existing phenomenon. (Isaac & Michael, 1981)

In this study the phenomenon includes the assistance and support experiences of beginning principals in learning needed information, determining the expectations for a given role, and understanding and adjusting to the operating norms of the school and district. . . . (Boullion, 1996)

Note that the researcher did not just give a definition of descriptive research from a noted authority, she also related the definition directly to her study and why it was appropriate for her study.

Population and Sample

The population and sample (or data sources) section includes a description of the individuals who participated in your study and the procedures used to select them. Ideally, an entire population would be used to gather information. However, this is usually not feasible as most groups of interest are either too large or are scattered geographically. When you don't have an opportunity to study a total group, select a sample as representative as possible of the total group in which you are interested. Gay and Airasian (1996) provided a clear definition of the terms *sampling* and *population* to help in distinguishing between the two:

Sampling is the process of selecting a number of individuals for a study in such a way that the individuals represent the larger group from which they were selected. The individuals selected comprise a sample and the larger group is referred to as a population. . . . The population is the group of interest to the researcher, the group to which she or he would like the results of the study to be generalizable. (pp. 111–112)

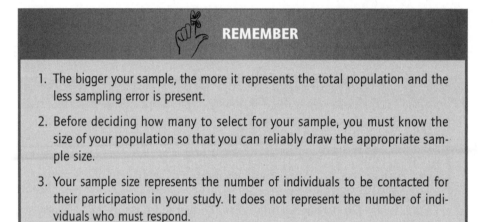

REMEMBER

1. The bigger your sample, the more it represents the total population and the less sampling error is present.

2. Before deciding how many to select for your sample, you must know the size of your population so that you can reliably draw the appropriate sample size.

3. Your sample size represents the number of individuals to be contacted for their participation in your study. It does not represent the number of individuals who must respond.

Sampling Procedures

Your study's credibility relies on the quality of procedures you used to select the sample. These procedures should be described in detail since they determine the generalizability of your findings. Your description should include the following:

1. The specific type of sampling used, such as probability sampling (random, systematic, stratified, cluster) or nonprobability sampling (purposive, expert)

2. The number of individuals included and where they are located

3. Why you selected this particular number and the unit of analysis

4. The criteria you used for inclusion in the sample

5. A step-by-step account of exactly how you went about selecting your sample

Following is an example from a dissertation of one way to describe sampling and rationale for criteria selection:

EXAMPLE

The population for this study consisted of forty-six (46) elementary schools in California implementing one of three national school reform projects.... Purposive sampling was used to identify schools within the population that met specific criteria. The criteria for selection included

1. Schools in their first or second year of implementation of their selected national school reform project,

2. Schools where the current principal was also the principal at the time of initiating the national school reform project, and

3. Schools willing to participate in the study.

Rationale for Selection of Criteria

The rationale for selecting the first criterion was twofold. The ability of individuals to accurately recall information regarding the period of time prior to implementation of their reform project would be difficult after more than two years.... The second criterion is related to the role of the principal in initiating any change process.... Because this research study focused on reform projects that change the structure and culture of a school, having the same principal who was also the principal at the time of the initiation phase was necessary to this study. The third criterion suggests that each principal's willingness to participate is critical to this study. Since the design of this research involved detailed questionnaires, participants needed to be willing to take the time necessary to respond. (Chaffee, 1995)

Instrumentation

This section includes a description of all instruments used to collect data—questionnaires, interview schedules, observation forms, and so on. Each instrument should be described in detail in the methodology section. Provide the following information, as relevant:

1. Appropriateness of the instrument for your population and setting

2. The validity and reliability of the instruments (*Validity* is the degree to which your instrument truly measures what it purports to measure. In other words, can you trust that findings from your instrument are true? *Reliability* is the degree to which your instrument consistently measures something from one time to another. If you measured the same thing again, would you find the same results?)

3. How the instrument is administered and scored

4. Interrater reliability—a check on the consistency between raters, or between a rater and an expert (This information is necessary when measurement involves subjective interpretation, such as open-ended questions.)

5. Type of response categories—rating scales, check lists, ranking, and so on (If you develop a new instrument, you should also recount how it was developed and include a description of the field tests that were conducted and the subsequent revisions. Place in the appendix a copy of all instruments used, unless they are copyrighted.)

REMEMBER

Copyrighted instruments are not reproduced in a dissertation. If you wish to use copyrighted instruments, permission should be obtained in writing from the holder of the copyright.

Developing Your Own Instrument

If you are unable to locate a satisfactory instrument that adequately measures your study's variables or concepts, you may either modify an existing validated instrument or create your own instrument. It is appropriate to change the wording or eliminate questions when modifying an instrument for a different population. However, keep in mind that the changes you make may affect the reliability and validity of the instrument. If you modify an instrument, it is your responsibility to justify the changes made and to provide information about the reliability and validity of the revised instrument.

HELPFUL HINT

A good idea: When developing items for your instrument, it is critical that you align the items with your research questions to ensure that all research variables are adequately covered in your instrument. A good technique is to create a matrix in which you display your research questions on the left side and the questionnaire items on the right. The following shows an alignment matrix.

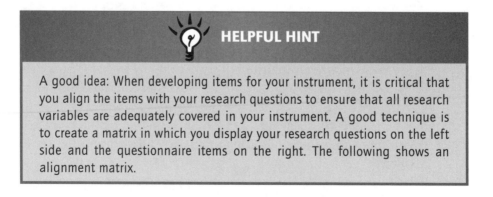

| Alignment of Research Questions and Variables With Questionnaire Items ||
Research Question and Variable	Questionnaire Item(s)
Research Question 1	Part II: Items 1, 2, 3, 4, 5
Variable A: Planning	
Research Question 1	Part II: Item 6
Variable B: Communicating the Change	
Research Question 1	Part II: Items 11, 12
Variable C: Visioning	
Research Question 1	Part II: Items 7, 8
Variable D: Decision Making	
Research Question 1	Part II: Item 9
Variable E: Managing Conflict	
Research Question 1	Part II: Items 10, 13
Variable F: Goal Setting	
Research Question 2	Part III: Item 14
Variable A: Advocacy From Central Administration	
Research Question 2	Part III: Item 15
Variable B: Teacher Advocacy	
Research Question 2	Part III: Items 16, 17, 18, 19, 20
Variable C: Access to Information	
Research Question 2	Part III: Items 21, 22, 23
Variable D: Community Pressure/Support/Apathy	
Research Question 2	Part III: Items 24, 25, 26
Variable E: New Policies and Funds	
Research Question 3	Part IV: Items 27, 28, 29, 30, 31
Variable A: Relative Advantage	
Research Question 3	Part IV: Items 32, 33
Variable B: Compatibility	
Research Question 3	Part IV: Items 34, 35
Variable C: Complexity	

When describing your instrument(s), it is important to explain your rationale for selection. Following is an example of such a paragraph that appeared in a dissertation:

EXAMPLE

In an exhaustive review of the literature, the research supporting the use of the SACQ far outweighed the criticism of the assessment tool. The SACQ has been used as an assessment tool in more than one hundred dissertations and theses. Even with its limitations, the majority of the research supported the use of the SACQ in understanding student adjustment to college. (Schultz, 2008, p. 110)

Following this rationale statement, the student then described his instrument's norms, reliability, and validity.

Field Testing

Any time you create your own instrument or modify an existing one, it must be field tested. You can select from five to 10 people to test the instrument and to make judgments about its validity. The people selected should not be involved in the study but should be like those in the study. Look for the following in pretesting an instrument:

- Understandable instructions
- Clear wording
- Adequate answers
- Sufficient detail
- Regional differences
- Difficult sections
- Irrelevant questions
- Length
- Convenience

Following is another example of how a dissertation student obtained feedback from field testing an online survey instrument. In his dissertation, he wrote:

The web-based questionnaire was administered to eighteen student employees who, after completing the questionnaire online, were asked to provide feedback on access to and navigation within the survey, technical difficulties experienced, clarity of instructions, typographical or grammatical errors, and general observations. The field test results and test participant feedback supported the validity and clarity of the survey and data collection method (see appendix A) (Schultz, 2008, p. 116).

Schultz (2008) asked respondents to respond to these questions about their field test experience:

1. Overall, how easy was it for you to access the survey and navigate from page to page?

2. Please describe any technical problems that you encountered while attempting to access or navigate from page to page.

3. Were the directions clear and easy to understand? If not, how can they be made easier for first-time students?

4. Were there any typographical errors that you discovered?

5. Please share any other comments or suggestions you may have that would help make this survey more successful. (pp. 204–207)

Following the field test, it is usually necessary to revise your instrument to reflect the various recommendations from the field test respondents. Be sure to state in this section what revisions were made to your instrument. The examples that follow should help to clarify these directions:

EXAMPLE 1

A pilot study was conducted in one of the districts selected for the sample. Within that district, two elementary schools that were not included in the sample were chosen for the pilot. The principals were selected because they had been implementing shared decision a minimum of one year and were willing to cooperate in the study. . . . The principals were interviewed using the Interview Guide. The researcher selected one teacher and one parent from the leadership team for individual interviews. All six sessions were tape recorded with permission of the participants. . . . Appropriate changes were made in the instrument to clarify the questions and to provide an easier format for recording answers for purposes of limiting the data to that which was most pertinent to the study. Question six was expanded to include more prompts, and clarified to include no more than three of the groups most involved in the decision making process. Question ten was expanded to. . . . (Walkington, 1991)

EXAMPLE 2

The modified interview schedule was field tested using five beginning principals from outside the central coast region in California who were first-year principals during the 1992–1993 school year. The field test utilized telephone interviews to simulate the actual data collection process. In addition to responding to the interview schedule, these principals gave feedback on the interview schedule by answering the following questions:

1. Is the interview schedule too long? (If yes, what would you suggest be dropped?)

2. Are the directions and wording clear and unambiguous? (If not, please note directions or words that are unclear.)

3. Is the format conducive to ease of response?

4. Do some of the questions need to be rephrased or dropped?

5. Are there additional questions that I should ask? (If yes, which questions would you suggest?)

As a result of the field test, no substantive changes were made to the interview schedule. Only minor modifications in wording were needed to make the questions flow more smoothly during the interviews. (Boullion, 1996)

Response Rate

The following questions are often asked by doctoral students conducting a questionnaire study:

1. What is an acceptable response rate for questionnaires?

2. How can I increase my response rate?

A major disadvantage of questionnaire studies is a low response rate, typically much lower than for personal interviews. Response rates for personal interviews are about 95%, whereas mail survey return rates are usually between 20% and 40%. The rule of thumb regarding an appropriate response rate is as follows:

Below 50% there is no defense

Below 60% is questionable but could be OK

You should try for 70% or above

There are several strategies you can employ to improve your response rate. Some examples are as follows:

1. Send a letter of endorsement by someone with whom the respondent can identify.

2. Use a professional-looking form.

3. Prepare an introductory letter that sells the respondent on the legitimacy and value of your study, its benefit to him or her, and guarantees of confidentiality and a copy of the results.

4. Offer inducements to respond. Appeal to the respondent's goodwill and altruism by stating you need his or her help. Other methods include such things as offering lottery tickets, a raffle prize, a $1.00 bill, a tea bag, and so on enclosed with the questionnaire form.

Probably the most effective method to increase your response rate is to use follow-ups such as a reminder postcard sent five days after the questionnaire. To those who don't respond, approximately two weeks later send a second follow-up that includes another reminder letter and a replacement questionnaire with a return envelope. After approximately two months, you can send by certified mail another letter and replacement questionnaire.

Data Collection Procedures

This section describes in detail all of the steps taken to conduct your study and the order in which they occurred. It is important that your writing is clear and precise so that other researchers can replicate your study. Your description should state how and when the data were collected. The following example from a dissertation describes one way to report data collection procedures:

EXAMPLE

Data collection began in September of 1995 and was completed by October. On September 9, 1995, surveys (Appendix C) were mailed to the eighteen (18) principals of the schools in the sample population. Each of the 18 principals received a telephone call from the researcher on September 9, 1995, to inform them that the survey was in the mail, and that they would be asked to complete and return it within one week. A cover letter was included describing the purpose of the research (Appendix C). Respondents were assured that neither their personal identity nor the identity of their school would be released in the dissertation.... Principals were asked to complete and return the survey to the researcher within one week. Principals who had not responded within two weeks received a follow-up telephone call from the researcher.... By October 26, 1995, there were a total of sixteen completed surveys, an 89 percent response rate. (Chaffee, 1996)

> **REMEMBER**
>
> Since sampling procedures were described in the "Sample and Population" section and your measures explained in the "Instrumentation" section, you do not need to repeat this information in this section.

> **HELPFUL HINT**
>
> A good idea: To help you efficiently deal with organizing data collection, create a Source of Data Chart. This chart keeps track of each data source in your study (e.g., who was interviewed, who received questionnaires, and what documents were analyzed). It also organizes the data sources by your research questions. See Appendix B for an example of a Source of Data Chart.

Best Time to Collect Data

When to collect data is a critical issue because it can greatly affect your response rate. It is important for you to consider the availability of your population. For example, in education there are several windows of opportunity when people are available. September, Christmas, and June are not the best times given the typical school calendar of events. Your best opportunity to collect data is usually October through November and January through April. These dates can vary if the school system is on a year-round schedule because people are "off track" throughout the school year.

Data collection always takes longer than you realize. A rule of thumb is to set a reasonable timeline, then double it! It takes time to schedule interviews, field test, travel, and follow-up on non-respondents. Refer to Appendix C for an example of a participant letter and questionnaire.

Data Analysis

This section includes an explanation of how you analyzed the data as well as your rationale for selecting a particular analysis method. If your study is quantitative, report the descriptive or inferential statistical tests and procedures you used, how they were treated, and the level of statistical significance that guided your analysis. Since statistical tests may vary by research question, you should explain your tests and procedures for each question. An example follows.

> Research questions four through nine focused on the differences in students' attitudes in looped and conventional classrooms. Composite means and standard deviations were computed for each of the attributes: self-concept, motivation, instructional mastery, and sense of control. The data were analyzed using *t*-test computations to determine if a significant difference existed between students in looped and conventional classrooms on each of the attitudes assessed. (Johnston, 2000)

If your study is qualitative, provide a description of matrices used to display the data and identify the coding processes used to convert the raw data into themes or categories for analysis. Your description should include specific details about how you managed the large amount of data associated with qualitative analysis. Include information about use of software, sticky notes, index cards, or other processes used. This helps readers understand how you reduced or transformed the data.

Every researcher approaches the coding process differently. There is no one right way to code textual data. One excellent guide to help you understand the coding process is provided by Tesch (1990). He described, in eight steps, a systematic process to analyze textual data:

1. Get a sense of the whole. Read all the transcriptions carefully. Perhaps jot down some ideas as they come to mind.

2. Pick one document (e.g., one interview)—the most interesting one, the shortest, the one on the top of the pile. Go through it asking yourself, "What is this about?" Do not think about the "substance" of the information but its underlying meaning. Write thoughts in the margin.

3. When you have completed this task for several informants, make a list of all topics. Cluster together similar topics. Form these topics into columns that might be arrayed as major topics, unique topics, and leftovers.

4. Now take this list and go back to your data. Abbreviate the topics as codes and write the codes next to the appropriate segments of the text. Try this preliminary organizing scheme to see if new categories and codes emerge.

5. Find the most descriptive wording for your topics and turn them into categories. Look for ways of reducing your total list of categories by grouping topics that relate to each other. Perhaps draw lines between your categories to show interrelationships.

6. Make a final decision on the abbreviation for each category and alphabetize these codes.

7. Assemble the data material belonging to each category in one place and perform a preliminary analysis.

8. If necessary, recode your existing data. (pp. 142–145)

The following example illustrates how one dissertation student explained her coding process. She describes a five-step process for analyzing interview transcripts. This process involved going from a holistic perspective to individual parts and back to a holistic look at the data.

EXAMPLE
Step 1: Initial Reading of Transcripts
After all thirty-one tape-recorded interviews were transcribed, the researcher reviewed all the data twice before developing a preliminary list of categories, themes, and patterns. Several prominent themes emerged from the initial reading. Each theme was given an initial coding.
Step 2: Organization and Coding of Responses
Next, the responses were sorted and grouped by research question. The researcher read through all the responses for each research question, highlighting pertinent information, and developed a master coding list of response categories (see Appendix F). Within each research question, response categories were counted by frequency.
Step 3: Review of Total Transcripts and Final Coding
Using the master coding list developed in Step 2, the researcher coded the full transcript of each participant, noting when second or third references were made in a response category. The coding list was then finalized.
Step 4: Completion of Data Analysis and Report of Findings
The analysis of each response to research questions and analysis of each interview transcript were conducted. This resulted in themes, patterns, and categories for the research questions.
Step 5: Review of Total Transcript to Ascertain Validity of Findings
The researcher reviewed all the transcripts a final time to ascertain that the findings and the main themes and patterns were consistent with the data. A comparison of the literature was made to determine which findings were supported or not supported by the literature. (Boullion, 1996)

A variety of qualitative software products are available for analyzing qualitative data; however, they do take time to learn how to use them well. A book titled *Computer Programs for Qualitative Data Analysis* by Weitzman and Miles (1995) offers guidance in learning the various software programs.

Validating the Findings

In this section on data analysis, it is important to include how you addressed the issue of validity. Qualitative researchers often use the term *trustworthiness* to refer to the concept of validity. It's the credibility factor that helps the reader trust your data analysis. For example, in qualitative studies, techniques such as triangulation, member checks, and interrater reliability are used to validate findings. Following is an example of how to report the process used to establish interrater reliability:

EXAMPLE

Interrater reliability is established through a process in which two or more people independently analyze the same qualitative data and then compare the findings. This process of multiple analysis reduces the potential bias of a single researcher collecting and analyzing the data (Patton, 1990). An expert practitioner in the socialization of elementary principals as well as in content analysis of qualitative data analyzed six transcripts from the interview data. The researcher and the expert analyzed the same six transcripts. Both the researcher and the expert used the research questions as a conceptual framework in analyzing the data. The researcher found thirteen common themes, patterns, and categories while the expert found twelve. These findings were the same 92 percent of the time. (Boullion, 1996)

Here is an example of how one researcher reported triangulated data. She validated interview information with archival data.

EXAMPLE

In addition to the responses from the interviews, the case data from archival records such as board policies, memos, newsletters, and other such documents were reviewed. These records were reviewed to validate or extend the statements made by the superintendents or the stakeholders in each of the districts. (Butt, 1993)

This example explains the process of validating case study findings by obtaining feedback from respondents:

EXAMPLE

To further validate the findings, drafts of each case report were submitted to the coordinator at each school site. They each reviewed the presentation of data for their site. There was overwhelming concurrence with the researcher's findings. Based on the comments from the coordinators, minor corrections were made regarding the titles of personnel delivering services, the use of funds, and the responsibilities of staff. There was also clarification of a factor that impeded services at one site and an addition to the factors impeding the delivery of services at another site. (Kinley, 1996)

REMEMBER

When explaining how you handled your data, be sure to relate how it was reported—standardized scores, raw data, percentages, mean, median, and so on. Also state how it was displayed—matrices, tables, graphs, charts, figures, or narrative text.

Limitations

Limitations are particular features of your study that you know may negatively affect the results or your ability to generalize. Limitations are usually areas over which you have no control. Some typical limitations are sample size, methodology constraints, length of the study, and response rate.

All studies have some limitations, and it is important that you state them openly and honestly so that people reading your dissertation can determine for themselves the degree to which the limitations seriously affect the study. Following is an example that describes the limitations of sample size and methodology:

EXAMPLE 1

The major limitation of the study is the relatively small sample size. Six districts and twelve schools were selected for the study. The source of information used to obtain this sample may not be complete. This may affect the generalizability of the study to other districts.

Another limitation is the use of the observation method. There is a possibility of observer bias anytime data are obtained from observations. (Walkington, 1991)

EXAMPLE 2

1. This descriptive study was limited to participants' self-reported perceptions of their experiences adjusting to college.

2. Individual results are based on a volunteer sample and do not necessarily define the population to which the individuals belong.

3. Since there were only six participants from the __ campus, the findings may not be generalized to that campus.

4. The SACQ provides a snapshot measurement of participants' self-reported perceptions. Their emotional state may be at a unique point given the survey was administered during the last three weeks of participants' first college semester. (Schultz, 2008, p. 119)

The following section offers a checklist of the elements to include in your methodology chapter.

Checklist of Elements to Include in the Methodology Chapter

After you have written your first draft of the methodology chapter, check off the following elements. Mark your draft where each of these elements is located.

Research Design

_____ Type of research

_____ Rationale for selection

_____ Appropriateness to your study

Population and Sample or Participants

_____ Description of respondents

_____ How many

_____ Where they are located

_____ Rationale for selection

_____ Size of population or sample

_____ Criteria for inclusion

_____ Specific type of sampling used

_____ Step-by-step sampling procedures

Instrumentation

_____ Detailed description of all instruments

_____ Type of response categories

_____ Appropriateness of instruments to your study

_____ Information on validity

_____ Information on reliability

_____ How instruments are administered and scored

_____ Interrater reliability procedures

_____ Criteria for judging competence

_____ How agreements will be assessed

_____ Percentage of data checked for agreement

_____ Statistics used to calculate agreement

_____ Field test or pilot test

_____ Describes test respondents

_____ How many

_____ Where located

_____ Feedback questions

_____ Reactions of respondents

_____ Procedures followed

_____ Revisions made to instruments

_____ Response rate

_____ Procedures used to increase response rate (e.g., follow-up methods)

Data Collection Procedures

_____ How data were collected

_____ When data were collected

_____ Where data were collected

_____ Procedures stated in order of occurrence

Data Analysis

_____ Includes how data were reported *and* displayed

_____ Provides information on validity and reliability of data (trustworthiness if a qualitative study)

_____ Explains methods used to analyze data

_____ States rationale for use of analysis techniques

Limitations

_____ Limitations stated

Summary

Selecting a methodology requires understanding the two major research paradigms: qualitative and quantitative approaches. Which one you select depends primarily on the problem investigated, the purpose of your study, and the nature of the data. Qualitative studies generate words that describe people's actions, behaviors, and interactions, whereas quantitative studies generate numbers derived from questionnaires, tests, and experiments. Often both approaches are combined in a single study, resulting in greater breadth and depth.

By describing your methodology clearly and precisely, you will make it possible for other researchers to adequately judge the worth of your findings and replicate your study. You must include detailed descriptions about your research design, population and sample, sampling procedures, instrumentation, data collection procedures, data analysis, and limitations.

Now that you completed your introductory and methodology chapters, it is time to meet with your committee to discuss and critically analyze your proposed study. The next chapter provides some guidelines for holding the proposal meeting.

13

Holding the Proposal Meeting

The proposal meeting represents a major step in the dissertation process. You and the entire committee meet to discuss and critically analyze your proposed study. Important understandings that will determine the ultimate direction of your research and the efficiency with which your study can be completed are reached at this meeting. Your goal is to obtain your committee's approval to move ahead with your study in accordance with agreements made in the meeting. Most universities require committee signatures on a document that becomes an informal contract between you and your committee. You agree to conduct the study as described in the proposal, and the committee agrees to grant you the doctorate after you finish.

Acceptable proposals vary according to the preferences of universities and dissertation advisors. At my university, proposals usually consist of the introductory and methodology chapters, an outline of the literature chapter, a bibliography, and the proposed research instruments to be used in the study. Whether or not you write the proposal in the future or past tense depends on your university's policy and the advisor's preference. Writing proposals in the past tense keeps you from having to adjust the tense in making the transition to the dissertation document.

Before the Meeting

Scheduling a proposal meeting involves (1) finding a date and time acceptable to all committee members, (2) selecting an appropriate and convenient location for the meeting, and (3) reserving the meeting room.

To ensure that committee members have adequate time to review your proposal before the meeting, it is preferable that they receive a final draft at least two weeks prior to the meeting. This draft should incorporate all of their ideas and recommendations for change. It should also be a high-quality document—clean, accurate, and complete.

To prepare yourself, consult your advisor about the proposal meeting's purpose and procedures. Also consult colleagues experienced in the process and get their perspective about the meeting's dynamics and expectations. I also advise that you be well steeped in the literature related to your topic. Not only does it give you greater self-assurance, it indicates to your committee that you understand and have control over your study's parameters.

🔆 HELPFUL HINT

Bring a buddy with you to take notes during the meeting. This allows you to interact freely in the discussion and to concentrate more fully on the recommendations being made by committee members. Even if a buddy is available, I suggest that you audio record the meeting so there is no doubt in your mind about what was said. Listening to the tape helps you to understand more clearly what committee members expect you to do as next steps.

During the Meeting

Your advisor typically introduces the committee members and facilitates the proposal meeting. Most meetings are informal in nature—characterized by a spirit of collegiality and support. Questions and comments about the proposal revolve around understanding the study, clarifying ambiguities, anticipating problems, and uncovering any major flaws in the study's design. The committee's role is to bring a new set of eyes to your study and help you define the parameters more clearly and precisely. Before your committee accepts your proposal and sends you off to gather data, committee members should agree on the following four things:

1. *The scope of inquiry.* Is it manageable? Is it dissertation-level research?

2. *Appropriateness of the design.* Is it suitable to the research questions asked? Is it doable?

3. *Significance of the study.* Does it make a valuable contribution to the field?

4. *Instrumentation.* Does your instrument(s) adequately cover the research questions asked?

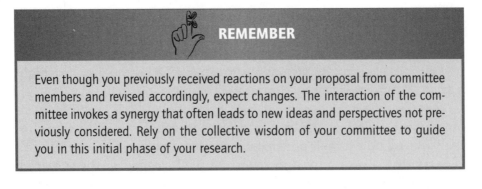

REMEMBER

Even though you previously received reactions on your proposal from committee members and revised accordingly, expect changes. The interaction of the committee invokes a synergy that often leads to new ideas and perspectives not previously considered. Rely on the collective wisdom of your committee to guide you in this initial phase of your research.

The proposal meeting is a good time to discuss and agree on the expectations and procedures to which you will adhere during the remainder of the study. By agreeing on the following, your work together should be smoother, more efficient, and less ambiguous.

1. When will drafts of chapters be submitted to committee members? Should you wait until the advisor approves each chapter before submitting them to the committee? Is it best to submit whole chapters or parts of chapters? Is it OK to work on other chapters while waiting?

2. How will chapters be submitted? By fax, mail, e-mail? If by mail, should a stamped, self-addressed envelope accompany each draft?

3. When can you expect drafts to be returned? One week, two weeks, whenever?

4. Should previous drafts be returned along with present ones? Is it necessary to indicate corrections in some way (boldfaced, colored highlighter, italics)?

5. Is it OK to phone if you have questions or concerns? What times are most convenient?

6. How should you manage feedback from committee members? Is it necessary to discuss suggestions made by the committee members with your advisor before incorporating them in the dissertation? What will you do if committee members make contradictory recommendations?

7. Is it appropriate to hire an outside consultant (editor, statistician, etc.)?

8. Are you expected to adhere faithfully to your timeline for completion or do you have some leeway based on extenuating circumstances?

At the proposal meeting's conclusion, the advisor usually summarizes the committee's decisions and recommendations for changes. This ensures understanding about what was said and agreed on.

After the Meeting

Immediately following the proposal meeting, you should confer with your advisor to interpret and reaffirm the committee's decisions and recommendations. This is the time to compare notes and get a complete understanding of what transpired at the meeting. It is especially important if substantive changes are required. At this time, you should review your timeline with your advisor and discuss any changes based on the outcomes of the proposal meeting.

Summary

Holding the proposal meeting represents a vital step in the dissertation process. At this meeting, you and your committee discuss your proposed study relative to its scope, design, instrumentation, and significance. You also agree on expectations and procedures for the study's duration.

You are now ready to make final preparations for the peak. This involves analyzing and presenting the results of your study. The next chapter guides you in understanding the data and how to present your findings.

PART V

Final Preparations for the Peak

14

Analyzing and Presenting the Results

You have gathered your interview, survey, test, archival, and observation data and are ready to make additional headway up the mountain—analyzing and presenting the results of your study. Specific data analysis techniques are beyond the scope of this book; the references in the Further Reading section at the end of this chapter will help you through your analytical trek.

The purpose of the results chapter is to report the findings of your study as clearly and succinctly as possible. Usually, you present findings in a narrative format supplemented by tables or figures. Tables display numerical data in rows and columns, whereas figures include any illustration other than a table (graphs, charts, diagrams, photographs, etc.).

As a general rule, the findings from your study should be presented objectively and without editorializing or speculating—free from author bias. *Dragnet* Sergeant Joe Friday's "Just the facts, ma'am, just the facts!" is appropriate. Occasionally, data interpretation is merged with the findings. Consult with your study advisor to ascertain his or her preference regarding this issue.

Understanding the Data

A Quantitative Study

Using Computer Printouts

If you use computer printout data, be sure to carefully peruse each page prior to creating tables or writing the narrative. Following are some practical suggestions from James Cox (1996) on beginning the analytic process.

1. Obtain *two identical sets of computer printouts*. Store one for future reference and *reorganize the other by research question*. This keeps your analysis focused. Get a manila folder for each research question. Then cut up your computer printout and physically place into the folders all relevant data pertinent to each research question. When you want to consider a particular research question, all the data pertinent to that question are in one folder. Information that does not directly address a research question can be saved in a separate folder.

2. Another process that won't mutilate your printout is to use colored markers to color-code the printout data. Use a different color for each research question and, as you peruse the printout, highlight those data directly related to each research question. You can then easily find the information for each of your research questions.

3. Know how to read your printout. Know what the numbers mean, which are relevant, and which are unimportant. Sit down with your statistician (if you hired one) and go over every aspect of your data, research question by research question. *If you're paying a statistician for his or her expertise, arrange up front that interpretation is part of the service.*

A Qualitative Study

Analyzing Themes and Patterns

If you are analyzing qualitative data (e.g., interview transcripts, observations, archival data), take time to become thoroughly familiar with your data—to make sense of what people said and to integrate what different respondents said. Analyzing qualitative data requires that you read through all your interview notes and transcriptions from beginning to end several times. Only then can you realistically generate categories, themes, and patterns that emerge from the data. A description of one coding process for developing themes and patterns is provided in Chapter 12 in the "Data Analysis" section. Similarly, observation data and analysis of archival data should be analyzed for emergent themes and patterns.

Writing the Introductory Paragraph

Begin this chapter with an introductory paragraph. Open with a sentence that briefly describes the problem and then explain the chapter's organization. Glatthorn (1998) provided an illustration of what you might write:

> As stated in Chapter 1, the study reported here examined in detail the problems encountered by teachers as they developed and used performance assessments in their planning and teaching. The chapter is organized in terms of the two specific research questions posed in Chapter 1. It first reports the problems they encountered in developing performance assessments; it then examines the difficulties they experienced in using those assessments in their teaching. (p. 165)

The introductory paragraph is often followed by a demographic description of the participants (gender, age, experience, etc.). These may be written or presented in table format.

Tables and the Narrative Description

Now it is time to create your tables and accompanying narrative to tell the story of your findings. How well the tables and narrative support each other affects the quality of your communication. It is important that your tables or figures are clear, concise, and easy to read. Also, remember to locate tables and figures as closely as possible to the text that discusses them.

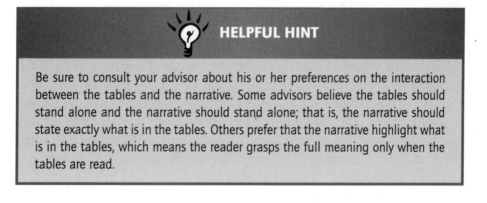

HELPFUL HINT

Be sure to consult your advisor about his or her preferences on the interaction between the tables and the narrative. Some advisors believe the tables should stand alone and the narrative should stand alone; that is, the narrative should state exactly what is in the tables. Others prefer that the narrative highlight what is in the tables, which means the reader grasps the full meaning only when the tables are read.

Plan Before You Write

The first question to ask yourself is, "Should my data be reported as a table, graph, diagram, chart, and so on, or should they simply be described in writing?" One helpful approach in planning this chapter is to create all your tables or figures before you do any actual writing. This makes the writing task much easier. Plus, taking time to arrange and report your data in different forms and in different ways (tables, etc.) stimulates your thinking and helps you to discover surprises or trends you might have overlooked. The information contained in these tables or figures helps you clarify the data and provides the basis for writing the narrative.

Presenting the Findings

Your presentation of findings depends on the nature of your research. A variety of organizational strategies are available from which to choose. For example, you can organize your data chronologically, by variable, by hypotheses, by research questions, by themes and patterns, or by any other approach appropriate for your study. Too often, students erroneously use questionnaire responses as their organizational structure.

Organizing your data by research question is a good way to clearly discuss your findings and to maintain consistency among chapters. The research questions become the headings—not necessarily the research question itself, but rather a heading that describes the question. Then, under each heading, present all the findings related to that question—the narrative and the various statistical analyses.

Qualitative Data

Qualitative data are usually presented in narrative form. Information is organized into themes, categories, or patterns. Often accompanying the narrative are tables that complement and simplify large amounts of information.

Qualitative analysis is a creative process and requires thoughtful judgments about what is significant and meaningful in the data. Confer with your advisor and committee members about how to present the rich data that flow from qualitative procedures. In the Further Reading section are two excellent books, Merriam (2001) and Miles and Huberman (1994), to guide you in coding and presenting qualitative data.

HELPFUL HINT

After writing the results from your first research question, first case, first hypothesis, and so on, send it to your advisor for approval. Obtaining approval of the style and format at this early stage saves you endless hours of rewriting. Plan on creating five to six drafts (even if you were class valedictorian). Always, always, always have someone who is objective read this chapter before sending it to your advisor. Clarity and precision are essential, and objective readers provide valuable assistance.

Guidelines for Designing Tables and Figures

Specific guidelines are required in developing and presenting graphic information. Carefully review your editorial style manual for detailed information and examples of the method and format for each kind of graphic. Following are some "be sure tos" for creating effective tables from Cox (1996), author of *Your Opinion, Please!*

- Write table titles that report exactly what is in the table.
- Label every column and every row.
- Avoid using too many numbers.
- Report group sizes (and avoid reporting percentages for small groups).
- Keep percents to tenths (in many instances, whole numbers will suffice).
- The key question is, "Can the tables stand alone?" (p. 49)

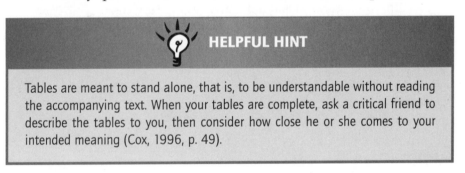

HELPFUL HINT

Tables are meant to stand alone, that is, to be understandable without reading the accompanying text. When your tables are complete, ask a critical friend to describe the tables to you, then consider how close he or she comes to your intended meaning (Cox, 1996, p. 49).

See Appendix D for an example of a table from a dissertation. For a more thorough discussion of how to analyze and report data in a clear, concise, and practical manner, read *Your Opinion, Please!* (Cox, 1996).

Concluding Paragraph

Write a paragraph that summarizes all of your key findings and explains what you discovered. Then direct the reader to the following chapter.

Questions to Ask About the Presentation of Findings

1. Are the findings clearly presented?

2. Are the tables and figures (if any) well organized and easy to understand?

3. Does each table stand on its own without narrative explanation?

4. Do the tables use the format specified by your required style manual?

5. Are the important or notable data in each table and figure described in the text?

6. Are the tables and narrative effectively integrated without unnecessary repetition?

7. Are the findings reported accurately and objectively?

8. Is factual information separate from interpretation and evaluation?

9. Are the data organized by research questions?

10. Is there a summary of the key findings at the end of the chapter?

Further Reading

Cox, J. (1996). *Your opinion, please! How to build the best questionnaires in the field of education.* Thousand Oaks, CA: Corwin.

Isaac, S., & Michael, W. B. (1995). *Handbook in research and evaluation.* San Diego, CA: EdITS/Educational and Industrial Testing Services.

Merriam, S. (2001). *Qualitative research and case study applications in education.* San Francisco: Jossey-Bass.

Miles, M. B., & Huberman, A. M. (1994). *Qualitative data analysis: An expanded sourcebook.* Thousand Oaks, CA: Sage.

Patton, M. Q. (2002). *Qualitative research & evaluation methods* (3rd ed.). Thousand Oaks, CA: Sage.

Summary

This chapter presented some recommendations for analyzing and presenting the results of your study. General guidelines were presented for reading computer printouts, writing the opening paragraph, and designing and presenting tables with accompanying narrative. The chapter concluded with some questions to ask yourself about presenting findings and technical references.

The next chapter guides you through the process of summarizing and discussing the results.

15

Summarizing and Discussing the Results

You are now ready for the final ascent on the dissertation journey. It's time to write the last chapter and explain to your readers what your findings mean. The chapter usually begins with a brief summary of the entire study and then presents conclusions and recommendations about the topic. Since this chapter is written at the very end of the dissertation process, students often have little energy left to provide thoughtful, comprehensive interpretations of their findings. It often seems rather anticlimactic, yet in many ways, it is the dissertation's key chapter. It provides answers to the problem stated in Chapter 1, plus readers typically turn first to this chapter for a complete picture of the research. In other words, it is the bottom line.

Reflect on Findings

One way to get your second wind to write this chapter is to take time to reflect on the results and implications of your study. Don't rush this most important phase. For the reader, this is the most interesting aspect of your dissertation. Spend a few days away from your research to put it in perspective and gain deeper insights.

This is the point in the process where you shift from being an objective reporter to becoming an informed authority and commentator. No one should be closer to the focus of the study, its progress, and its data than you. You now have the responsibility to tell others about what your findings mean and to integrate your findings with current theory, research, and practice. Considerable thought and diligent reflection are required when interpreting research results.

 **HELPFUL HINT**

One way to reflect on your study prior to writing this chapter is to imagine giving a five-minute speech to a group of your peers or to a professional organization. In a few sentences, summarize what your study means. What three main conclusions would you share with the group?

Chapter Organization

This chapter will vary depending on your research methodology, your findings, and the preferences of your study advisor. There is no "right" way to organize this chapter. Consider discussing your study's meaning using creative alternatives that add interest for the reader. Some students generate interest through scenarios, letters, dialogues, stories, and profiles. A traditional Chapter 5 usually includes any combination of the following elements:

- Introduction
- Summary of the study
  - Overview of the problem
  - Purpose statement and research questions
  - Review of the methodology
  - Major findings
- Findings related to the literature
- Surprises
- Conclusions
  - Implications for action
  - Recommendations for further research
  - Concluding remarks

Introduction

Write a brief introductory paragraph that focuses the reader on the chapter's organization and content. Here is an example of what you might write:

This chapter presents a summary of the study and important conclusions drawn from the data presented in Chapter 4. It provides a discussion of the implications for action and recommendations for further research.

Summary of the Study

This section contains the summary of your study—a "mini version" of all previous chapters. It should stand alone as a description of your study and be sufficient in detail, without undue repetition, so the reader can grasp the entire study without referring to previous chapters.

Your summary should include a brief overview of the problem, the purpose statement, research questions, a review of the methodology, and a summary of the major findings. In the methodology review, it is appropriate to include the type of research, data collection procedures, and data analysis techniques.

Findings Related to the Literature

Relating your findings to the literature may be contained in the major findings section or in the conclusions section, or it may be emphasized as a separate section with its own heading. Wherever you decide to place this section, you are expected to describe the relationship of your study to the literature and to prior research. What are the differences between your study and previous studies? How do your findings compare with those in the literature? How do they fit or not fit into the findings of previous studies? Do your findings help clarify contradictions in the literature? Do your findings have any special importance, either as improvements over prior findings or in breaking new ground?

Your study may have implications for current theory. You may have found evidence that supports or negates existing theory. If so, point this out. It is important to clearly state the ways your study contributes to the current knowledge base.

Surprises

Surprises are the unanticipated outcomes of your study. What uncontrolled variables may have influenced the results? Surprises could occur within your sample, with the instrumentation used, in responses from participants, in test results, and so on. Provide the reader with your analysis of the unusual problems or surprising outcomes. You may choose to include this information in various sections or create a separate section to discuss these findings.

Conclusions

Webster defines a *conclusion* as "reasoned judgment . . . inference based on evidence . . . final summation." This is your chance to have the last word on the subject. Writing conclusions well relies on your ability to be a critical and creative thinker—to analyze, synthesize, and evaluate information. Drawing conclusions from findings pushes you to consider broader issues, make new connections, and expand on the significance of your findings. You are granted considerable leeway to express your own voice—to be flamboyant in stating your opinions about your findings. However, you are required to make plausible explanations, speculate, and draw conclusions warranted by your findings. Your conclusions cannot be subjective opinions.

Both your problem statement and your literature review were organized to lead the reader from a broad general view of the topic area to specific issues that became the focal point of your study. In this section, you can reverse that approach and lead the reader from the particular findings of your study toward generalized interpretations of those findings.

HELPFUL HINT

When discussing or explaining results, be careful about choosing your words. Use qualifiers such as *seems, appears, possible, probably, likely,* or *unlikely* when addressing causality, suggesting explanations, generalizing to a larger population, or identifying reasons why certain events occurred in the study.

REMEMBER

1. One conclusion may cut across more than one finding.

2. Don't confuse results and conclusions. Results are "just the facts," whereas conclusions represent a higher level of abstraction—going beyond mere facts to higher levels of interpretation, analysis, and synthesis of results. So don't just restate the research findings.

3. All conclusions must be backed up by your data.

4. Don't add anything in this section not previously presented in the results chapter.

5. "Avoid melodramatic or intemperate language such as 'amazing' or even 'interesting' or 'important.' Allow your data and conclusions to be judged on their own merits and not on your amplification of them." (Rudestam & Newton, 1992, p. 124)

Implications for Action

More than likely, your findings have practical implications for professional practice. In Chapter 1, you included a section titled "Significance of the Study." While preparing for this significance section, you considered *who* will likely benefit from your study, *what* they will learn from it, and *why* they will gain from this knowledge. This section from Chapter 1 now becomes the basis for preparing your implications for action. In other words, what would you tell people to do differently as a result of your findings? *Remember that the actions you recommend must be based on your findings, not on personal biases.*

Recommendations for Further Research

You are expected to present recommendations for ways that your study can be improved upon and for how future studies might contribute to the field. These recommendations may arise from constraints imposed on your study, conditions you could not or chose not to control, or your insights regarding different populations, different questions, or further confirmation of your findings.

Concluding Remarks

Include a wrap-up statement that pulls together your comments and highlights the main points of the chapter. It is also appropriate to include some personal insights, beliefs, or inspirations derived from conducting your study.

**FINIS! CONGRATULATE YOURSELF AND
CELEBRATE WRITING YOUR LAST PARAGRAPH.**

Questions to Ask About Summarizing and Discussing the Findings

1. Is there a brief summary of the problem, the methodology, and the findings?
2. Are conclusions clearly stated?
3. Are conclusions derived from the findings?
4. Are conclusions mere restatements of the findings?
5. Are conclusions discussed within the framework of previous studies, theory, and the literature base?
6. Are generalizations made that are not warranted by the findings?

(Continued)

(Continued)

7. Are generalizations confined to the population from which the sample was drawn?

8. Are implications for action made that are not justified by the data?

9. Are recommendations for future research made?

Summary

Chapter 5 of your dissertation summarizes the entire dissertation and interprets the findings. Readers frequently turn to this chapter first to obtain a complete picture of the research. For that reason, suggestions on the content and organization of this final chapter were offered and a list of questions to help you reflect on what to include was provided.

Now for the final ascent! You now have the opportunity to defend your study. The next chapter offers guidelines about the oral defense meeting.

PART VI

Final Ascent and View From the Top and Beyond

Remember that what is hard to endure will be sweet to recall.

—Tote Yamada

Live your life each day as you would climb a mountain. An occasional glance toward the summit keeps the goal in mind. . . . Climb slowly, steadily, enjoying each passing moment, and the view from the summit will serve as a fitting climax for the journey.

—Harold V. Melchert

16

The Oral Defense

D-Day

It usually takes more than three weeks to prepare a good impromptu speech.

—Mark Twain

This is it! You are almost at the top. This ultimate step, the oral defense of your dissertation, is the culmination of your doctoral journey. You have worked long and hard and, hopefully, have produced a scholarly piece of work of which you can be proud. Your advisor and committee members also take pride and pleasure in your accomplishment.

This chapter was written to guide your thinking and to relieve some anxiety as you prepare for the oral defense. It explains the oral defense process by describing a typical defense scenario, the roles of the participants, and the pass/fail criteria. Helpful hints are included to assist in making your oral defense a pleasant and memorable experience.

This event provides the opportunity to speak publicly about your research study and to defend it. The oral defense is a long-standing tradition in academia. Its major purpose is to demonstrate your ability to advocate for and justify your research problem, methodology, findings, and conclusions. In today's academic environment, it is usually conducted in an informal setting. In most instances, it is an exciting, congenial, and pleasurable experience. Those present at the defense vary from one institution to another, but generally they include your advisor and other committee members, an outside reader representing the dean, and other interested academic community members and friends.

You should schedule your oral defense only when you, your advisor, and the committee are satisfied that your work is substantially complete and reflects the standards of high-quality research. Remember, not only your reputation is on the line but also that of your advisor, who has been the principal guide and evaluator of your work. It is important that you present to committee members the best possible final draft of your dissertation—free of grammatical and typographical errors. Allow at least two weeks for committee members to review the final copy of your dissertation.

In collaboration with your committee, arrange for the date, time, and place of the defense. The defense date should allow sufficient time (three weeks minimum) for the required procedures and approvals.

A Defense Scenario

What does an oral defense look like? Although the format and roles may vary from institution to institution and from advisor to advisor, most follow common procedures. Here is a scenario that represents a typical oral defense.

1. You arrive about 30 minutes early to arrange the room properly.

2. Your advisor facilitates the meeting, usually opening with introductions. He or she introduces the committee members, guests, and the outside reader. You then introduce any family or friends who are present.

3. Your advisor explains the purpose of the oral defense and the procedures to be followed in conducting the defense. Keep in mind your advisor is an ally to you and is in your corner at the defense.

4. You are asked to provide a brief overview of your study—not more than 5 to 15 minutes. The overview should include the following:
   a. The purpose of your study and the research questions
   b. What literature you found particularly helpful
   c. The methodology used (Include the population and sample, your instruments, and your process for data collection and analysis. Also include the rationale for selecting your sample and method of analysis.)

d. Major findings and conclusions from the findings

e. Recommendations you would make for action and further research

It's a good idea to present this summary without numerous notes. If PowerPoint presentations are used, keep the number of slides to a minimum. Just talk to the committee about your study.

5. Who asks the first question is a matter of advisor preference. Members of the committee ask their questions either randomly or systematically, chapter by chapter. Committee members should limit their discussion to matters of substance and special concerns rather than those relating to editorial issues. These may be provided at the end of the defense.

6. When committee members have finished with their questions, it is appropriate that visitors are invited to ask questions if they desire. This is a public oral defense. When there are no further questions, you and all visitors exit the room to allow time for the committee to deliberate and decide if you successfully defended and if your dissertation document is acceptable. A unanimous vote of all committee members is usually required to pass the oral defense.

7. The committee decides among the following:

a. Pass with no revisions

b. Pass with minor revisions (completed with the advisor's guidance)

c. Pass with major revisions (final approval by the committee)

d. Continue the oral defense

e. Fail

What is the difference between minor and major revisions? Minor revisions are those changes that require no substantial rewriting. Examples include updating the bibliography, correcting tables, adding more conclusions or recommendations, and correcting typographical and grammatical errors. Most minor revisions can be completed in a weekend, or a week at the most. Major revisions are those involving a substantial rewrite of particular sections. Major errors may be incorrect statistics, inconsistency between the research questions and findings, an outdated literature review, poor instrumentation, or lack of adequate data.

8. You and the visitors return. If you pass the oral defense, you receive hearty congratulations by all. You will remember that moment of supreme bliss when your advisor shakes your hand

and says, "Congratulations, Dr.____." As you reflect on your journey's experiences, you can probably relate to these amusing words: "Being a graduate student is like becoming all of the Seven Dwarves. In the beginning you're Dopey and Bashful. In the middle, you are usually sick (Sneezy), tired (Sleepy), and irritable (Grumpy). But at the end, they call you Doc, and then you're Happy" (Azuma, 2002, p. 2).

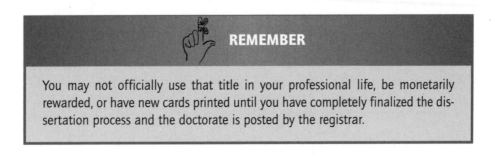

REMEMBER

You may not officially use that title in your professional life, be monetarily rewarded, or have new cards printed until you have completely finalized the dissertation process and the doctorate is posted by the registrar.

9. Discuss the revisions to be made with your advisor, and clarify procedures for final approval and sign-off. The whole process usually takes from one to two hours.

Helpful Hints: Prior to the Oral Defense

Following are some helpful hints for you to consider in the days prior to, during, and after the oral defense.

- Read your dissertation carefully so you can respond readily and authoritatively to the questions asked. Play devil's advocate with yourself and try to identify as many of your study's weaknesses as possible.
- Bring yourself up to date with recent work published that you may not have had time to read while writing the dissertation. The more familiar you are with the relevant literature in your field, the more you will appear as an expert.
- Try to anticipate what committee members will ask you. List the things you know you will be asked, and practice your responses. Also, list questions you would *hate* being asked and practice answering them.
- Do some deep reflections on the value of your dissertation to the field. Who are the people and groups that might profit from your findings? What additional recommendations would you make to these people?

- Probe yourself further about how your findings relate to the literature—both theoretical and practical.
- Prepare for questions about why you chose one method rather than another or one statistical procedure over another. Be sure you thoroughly understand any statistics used in your study. Even if you consulted a statistician for assistance in crunching the numbers and interpretation, you still are responsible for explaining your rationale and use of the selected statistical procedures.

  Here are some typical questions you might think about:
  - What were the surprises for you? The disappointments?
  - What brought you to explore this particular topic?
  - What did you learn about your subject area? About yourself?
  - What were your key learnings about research?
  - What does your study say to professionals in your field?
  - What is your assessment of the strengths and weaknesses of your study?
  - Were you to start over, would you do anything differently? If so, what?
  - What was the most significant aspect of the work you've done?
  - Since you wrote your literature review, have you noticed any new work published?

- Use the few weeks before your oral defense to continue contemplating your study. As you do this, you will have fresh insights and new "ahas" from time to time. Write them down and bring them to your oral defense to share with the committee.
- Look for errors—you will always find them—either typographical or in the data. Note what they are and bring a list to the defense. Your committee will appreciate your efforts to produce high-quality work.
- Talk to recent graduates and ask about their experiences and the questions they were asked.
- Attend other oral defenses, especially those conducted by your advisor. Seeing the oral defense in action relieves the mystery and angst surrounding it.
- Conduct a mock defense in which a group of your colleagues simulate an oral defense by acting as your committee. You will probably find their questions harder than those posed by the real committee. Be sure to build in time for feedback on your performance.

- Prepare a 5- to 15-minute overview of your dissertation and practice presenting it without notes.
- Practice. Practice. Practice.
- Get a good night's sleep and visualize your ideal oral defense.

During the Oral Defense

- Breathe deeply and stay calm! You want to appear relaxed and confident.
- Maintain eye contact while you are listening to, and answering, questions. Remember to smile occasionally. It has a positive effect on your committee and improves your mindset.
- You can have notes, a PowerPoint presentation, or transparencies—not too many, however. Trust yourself. You are more knowledgeable than anyone about your topic.
- Feel free to consult your dissertation; tabs for important sections may be helpful.
- Really listen to the questions. Don't jump to the conclusion that you know where the person is going and cut him or her off. Let the committee member state the entire question.
- Be appreciative of any criticisms and suggestions to improve your study. Acknowledge the critic's contribution.
- Expect to be asked questions that are not completely clear. When a question is asked that you do not completely understand, ask that the question be rephrased or restated.
- If a question is asked not related to your study, you might concede that it is an interesting question and would be an excellent topic for a follow-up study.
- Create some "think time" for yourself by
  - Counting to three before responding
  - Paraphrasing the question before answering (In other words, state the question in your own words. You don't want to answer the wrong question.)
- Try to formulate sharp, precise answers. It is better to answer the question first and then elaborate more if needed. Don't ramble, but don't be too brief either. After an answer, you might say: "Does that answer your question?" or "Would you like me to elaborate?"
- Sometimes a question requires a response that goes beyond the data or findings of your study. Feel free to express an opinion; however, be sure to label your response as such.

- If you find yourself in trouble, take a *time out* and go back to the beginning or take time to collect your thoughts. If you don't know the answer to a question, there is no harm in saying, "I don't know." It is better to tell the truth than to fake it. *Remember the proverb "When you find yourself in a hole, stop digging."* If you get totally flustered or overly emotional, simply ask for a break and get a drink or go to the restroom. This can help you regain your composure.

- The stronger your dissertation, the deeper the committee members may want to explore your findings. They might try to test your convictions about your conclusions and recommendations.

- Feel free to show enthusiasm for your study. After all, you spent tremendous amounts of time, energy, and money in conducting the research and preparing your dissertation.

- Consider bringing a tape recorder or having someone take notes for you. The notes should focus on the specific suggestions and changes that each committee member asks for. Comments should be labeled with the name of the person who requested the change or made a comment. Your advisor is the final arbitrator of changes to be made.

- Be sure to thank those in the room who helped you along this dissertation journey. This includes not only your committee members but also any family members and friends who supported you in this incredible endeavor.

REMEMBER

Remember These Encouraging Thoughts

1. You know more about your dissertation than anyone else. You are the expert on your topic. Your months of concentrated reading and research contributed to a unique knowledge of your topic that few others possess.

2. Everyone involved wants you to succeed. You completed a rigorous piece of research, and you should be proud to discuss it publicly.

3. Look forward to being welcomed into the community of scholars!

After the Oral Defense

- If your committee asks for revisions, get right on them. Don't lose any momentum. Usually, you can incorporate minor revisions in a weekend or a week. Major revisions take longer, depending on the issues involved. Be very clear about what needs to be altered. With minor revisions, the committee usually signs off and leaves your advisor with the responsibility to monitor the changes according to the committee's wishes.

- Find out the university's protocol for completion of the dissertation process.
- Celebrate this exhilarating experience with friends, colleagues, and loved ones. By all means, take pictures to record this memorable event.

Summary

The oral defense of your dissertation represents the culmination of your doctoral journey. It provides the opportunity to speak publicly about your research and to defend it. This chapter provided an overview of the process and some helpful hints for prior to, during, and after the oral defense. It can be an exhilarating experience for you, your committee, friends, and family. Now prepare for commencement—that special time when you stand on top of the mountain.

Like all mountain climbs, however, you must eventually descend. The next chapter discusses the let-down experience and ways you can mentor others as they attempt the same journey. This final chapter, titled "The Next Peak," helps you think about ways to disseminate your study's findings to the knowledge base in your field.

17

The Next Peak

You have climbed the mountain . . . now soar beyond!

—Mario Fernandez

Commencement! You now know what it is like standing on top of a high mountain. The view is awesome, and the exhilaration and pride of high achievement are unforgettable. It's a peak experience. This is the time for celebration, frivolity, and picture taking—rejoicing with friends, colleagues, and family. All those who supported you through this long, arduous journey can now revel in your accomplishments and share with you the grandeur of commencement.

Rejoice in commencement! It is a mountain-top experience worthy of celebration. Like all climbs, though, you must descend. The descent causes some students to experience an emotional letdown and feel a sense of loss. These are normal feelings caused by intense concentration and pressure for several years. During this time you return to a "normal" life and reacquaint yourself with family and friends.

The Descent

As all climbers must eventually descend the mountain and return to the valley floor, so too must dissertation writers return to normal life activities and reflect on future professional opportunities. Experienced mountaineers know that the descent can be difficult and rife with dangers. Doctoral students often report mixed feelings about completing their study, parting from friends with whom they bonded, and leaving the intellectual stimulation of the university. Some go through periods of depression and feelings of general malaise.

Letting Down

This emotional letdown is quite normal given the tremendous pressure and stress of trying to juggle one's personal and professional lives for several years. The dissertation is an overpowering presence that consumes all your attention. Even though there is a sense of relief in having it over, for most there is also a sense of loss. Making the transition to a normal life may take a while as you deal with the myriad feelings associated with starting anew.

After the dissertation, you have all these "extra hours." Take some time to regain your energy and indulge yourself in pleasurable pastimes so often sacrificed—hobbies, mystery books, movies, vacations, regular workouts, and so on. Certainly, it is a good idea to reacquaint yourself with family and friends who were probably quite neglected during your hours of isolated study.

Not only is it desirable to rebalance your personal life, but refocusing your professional agenda keeps your career moving ahead. After all, you probably decided to earn the doctorate to advance your career goals. You've invested several years and thousands of dollars to be called "doctor." How unfortunate if the scholarly work you produced gathers dust on a shelf, soon to be forgotten except for by those few future researchers who might stumble across it. Your research study added a new piece to the academic puzzle in your field and offers an opportunity for others to learn from your research.

Mount Analogue

Along the dissertation journey, you gained new knowledge and wisdom, honed some valuable skills, gained confidence in your abilities as a writer and scholar, and made lasting friendships. However,

> you cannot stay on the summit forever; you have to come down again. . . . So why bother in the first place? Just this: what is above knows what is below, but what is below does not know what is above. In climbing, always take note of difficulties along the way; for as you go up, you can observe them. Coming down you will no longer see them, but you will know they are there if you have observed them well.

One climbs, one sees. One descends, one sees no longer but one has seen. There is an art to conducting oneself in the lower regions by the memory of what one saw higher up. When one can no longer see, one can at least still know. (Daumal, 1952, p. 153)

Helping Others

In 1924, a French poet, Rene Daumal, wrote an allegorical novel titled *Mount Analogue*. The mountain symbolizes a spiritual voyage of discovery much like *Pilgrim's Progress*. As the adventurers in the story ascend the mountain, they discover strange, nearly invisible crystals called *paradama*, which are symbolic of rare and difficult truths found along the spiritual path. Daumal died before completing the novel but left these words about one of the basic laws of Mount Analogue: "To reach the summit, one must proceed from encampment to encampment. But before setting out for the next refuge, one must prepare those coming after to occupy the place one is leaving. Only after having prepared them, can one go on up" (Daumal, 1986, p. 104).

> To know the road ahead, ask those coming back.
>
> —Chinese proverb

You will have many more peaks to climb in your career and in your life. In this parable of Mount Analogue, Daumal (1924) exhorts us not to forget those who follow in our footsteps. Here are some ways in which you can mentor others as they attempt their journey to the top.

Mentoring

There is no greater gift to those who follow in your footsteps than being available to lend a helping hand as they attempt the dissertation journey. One way is to act as an on-the-job coach for doctoral students who work in your place of employment. Frequently, there are opportunities to help them apply course work to real situations, provide straight-scoop information about the challenges of dissertating, and offer encouragement and support when they falter along the path.

Disseminating Your Study's Findings

How better to help others than to contribute your study's findings to the knowledge base in your field. Every study builds on previous studies. If yours is not available to others, it can't be used to extend knowledge. Remember, you are now an expert, an authority on your subject, and expected to make wise judgments and recommendations in your special area.

It is natural to want to avoid even looking at your dissertation after working on it so hard and so long. However, letting it sit on the shelf for a long period of time risks never taking it to the next step of sharing your results with a wider audience. It also keeps you from taking full advantage of the professional opportunities it affords you. Instead of ignoring it permanently, take the time that you devoted each week to writing the dissertation and work on ways to disseminate your research and extend your professional network. Presenting your research, creating products, and publishing are ways to disseminate your findings.

Unfortunately, very few dissertations end up being published. In my experience, students are just plain worn out from their years of doctoral study—completing coursework and writing the dissertation. They often feel as if they neglected their family and themselves too long and want to get on with their lives. Very few take the time to do the major rewrites necessary to turn their dissertation into a publishing format. Nonetheless, presenting or publishing your results to a wider audience than your committee is one of the best ways to contribute knowledge to your field and advance your professional life.

Presenting Your Research

A good first step is to present your research to professional associations in your field and obtain feedback from the participants. Presentations can be made at regional, state, national, and international conferences. They are always on the lookout for presenters and are quite receptive to new and interesting findings in their field. Conference formats include presenting papers, participating in panel discussions and poster sessions, leading workshops, and making formal addresses. Scan your professional journals for "calls for papers," a formal invitation to submit an application to speak. When you submit a proposal, you receive guidelines about the length of the presentation and the required format. If you decide to pursue presenting your study at conferences, remember that submissions must be sent in months in advance of the conference.

In making a presentation to an audience of practitioners, Alan Glatthorn (1998) suggested this outline for a 30-minute time allocation:

1. What you learned: 2 minutes (a very general statement as an introduction)

2. Your methodology: 3 minutes

3. A detailed summary of your results: 5 minutes

4. Applications for practice: 20 minutes (p. 190)

Poster Sessions

Poster sessions advertise your research—usually at a conference or seminar. A poster is a visual layout that depicts your research study. Posters should be informative and artistic, a combination of text and graphics such as tables and graphs for a visually pleasing display. Your poster should contain only the crucial points of your research, such as

- Introduction
- Methods
- Results
- Discussion and conclusions
- Future directions
- Acknowledgments and references

Your goals in designing a poster are simplicity and clarity. You want to provide enough material to explain your research without an oral explanation and to initiate discussion and questions.

Presenting your poster at a conference usually involves making a short presentation (about 5–10 minutes) to give periodically to those assembled around your poster. Handouts may also be available for the participants. Oftentimes, you have an opportunity to engage in an in-depth discussion of your work.

Also consider presenting your research to interested public and civic organizations (Elks, Lions, etc.) or to your local board of education, PTA, trade group, or job associates. Perhaps your own university department might organize research forums for sharing dissertation results.

Publishing Your Research

You can publish your research either online, in a journal, as a chapter in an edited book or textbook, or as a book.

Online

An online option for publishing can be found with Dissertation.com. "The primary function of Dissertation.com is to provide students, researchers, and the general public with low cost access to important academic work. Our publications are made easily accessible on-line and through thousands of booksellers, reducing the cost of acquisition and speeding delivery to those interested" (http://www .dissertation.com).

Journal Article and Book

Your dissertation could also be the basis for a journal article or, possibly, for a book. More than likely, your chances are greater publishing a journal article rather than a book. Reworking a formal, technical, and usually boring dissertation into a reader-friendly book requires a major rewrite and a lengthy time commitment.

To initiate the process of publishing, I suggest that you first talk to your dissertation committee or published professors on campus for their advice on specific journals and how to approach them. Some might make a personal introduction to an editor he or she is familiar with. It is important that you find a journal that publishes articles that match your research topic and your particular study. Some journals focus on empirical research, while others publish theoretical or applied articles. You simply need to review the main journals in your field to get a sense about the type of articles they publish. Also, be aware that journals are rated in quality based on refereeing systems and how often they are cited by other researchers. Refer to the *Social Science Citation Index* and the *Arts and Humanities Citation Index* for determining the citation scores of most journals.

A next step might be to visit your university library and peruse all journals pertinent to your field of interest and potential audience. Each of the major journals provides information about how to submit manuscripts for consideration. Also consult your reference librarian about the available references on publishing in your field.

Third, invest in resources that provide detailed information on the publishing process from beginning to end. Following are two of these references:

Bolker, J. (1998). *Writing your dissertation in fifteen minutes a day.* New York: Henry Holt. (See chapter "Life After the Dissertation.")
Klausmeier, H. (2001). *Research writing in education and psychology—From planning to publication.* Springfield, IL: Charles C Thomas.

There are other resources recommended by these authors that greatly enhance your understanding of the publishing essentials.

Creating Products

Chapter 5 of dissertations usually contains a section titled "Implications for Action," in which the author makes concrete suggestions to practitioners in the field that are directly related to the study's findings. Frequently, recommendations are made to create specific products, such as new training programs, handbooks, manuals, new programs, and videos. Taking time to follow up on creating these products makes a practical and greatly appreciated contribution to the field.

Summary

Commencement is the joyous celebration of high achievement—a mountain-top experience. However, all climbers must eventually descend and return to normal life. Some experience an emotional letdown with feelings of loss—quite normal following such a long, arduous journey. This is the time to regain energy, indulge in pleasurable pastimes, and think ahead. Your next peak represents the opportunity to contribute to others as a mentor and contribute further to the knowledge base in your field. Some suggestions were offered in this chapter, such as (1) presenting your research at conferences as a presenter or in a poster session; (2) speaking about your research to various organizations; (3) publishing your research online, in journals, or in a book; and (4) creating products as follow-up to research recommendations.

Parting Thoughts

I hope you found the suggestions and approaches offered in this book useful and valuable on your journey to complete the dissertation. I also hope your journey is an enjoyable one and results in one of the most rewarding personal experiences of your life. I leave you with two simple but powerful thoughts.

Be positive! A positive mental attitude, more than any other factor, will determine whether you complete your dissertation or not. View obstacles as plateaus on the way to the summit and find ways to surmount them. Persistence and determination are what it takes to finish. Don't give up no matter how much it starts to hurt—just shift gears and keep going. Nothing great comes without a price.

> Success is never the result of spontaneous combustion. You must set yourself on fire.
>
> —Arnold Glasow

Get it done! Don't wait for inspiration. Develop a sense of urgency about completing your dissertation. No matter how brilliant or talented you are, if you don't have a sense of urgency, develop it now. Tomorrow is not a day of the week.

Good luck and God bless!

Appendix A: Sample Dissertation Timeline—Gantt Chart

Task Name	2010						2011												2012								
	J	A	S	O	N	D	J	F	M	A	M	J	J	A	S	O	N	D	J	F	M	A	M	J	J	A	S
Admission to Candidacy	◆																										
Select Advisor			█	█																							
Committee Approval					█	█																					
Study Proposal Approved							█	█	█	█																	
Data Collection															█	█											
Finish Chapters 1, 2, and 3								█	█	█	█	█	█	█	█	█											
Data Analysis																	█	█									
Write Chapter 4																		█	█								
Write Chapter 5																			█	█							
Approval for Oral Defense																				█	█						
Note Deadline for Oral Defense																						◆					
Oral Defense																					█	█					
Revisions and Committee Approval																						█					
Final Typing																							█	█			
Manuscript Review																								█	█		
Final Revisions and Approval																									█		
Dean Signs																										◆	
HELLO Dr.!																											☺

Appendix B

Source of Data Chart

Sample: A source of data chart was developed prior to the field test to assist with the comprehensive and efficient process of data collection. Each variable was explored through one or more of the following: interviews of students, teachers, administrators, and parents; archival document reviews; or classroom and school setting observations (Melendrez, 1991, p. 79).

Question/Variable	INT	ARC	OB	SOURCE
A. What are the historical origins of each specialized arts school?				
1. Original concept	X	X		ACD
2. Political issues	X	X		AC
3. Key people/groups	X	X		ACD
4. Length of planning period	X	X		ACD
5. Curriculum development	X	X		ACD
6. Start up funding	X			ATSD
B. What operational processes are in place at each school?				
7. Student recruitment/selection	X	X		ADH
8. Student demographics	X	X		AD
9. Staffing	X	X		AD
10. Staff recruitment/selection	X			AH

(Continued)

(Continued)

Question/Variable	INT	ARC	OB	SOURCE
11. Curriculum—academics	X	X	X	DHAV
12. Curriculum—arts	X	X	X	DHAV
13. Financial aspects	X	X		AD
14. Facilities	X		X	AV
15. Advisory councils	X			A
16. Public relations	X	X		AD

INT = Interview

ARC = Archival documents

OB = Observation

SOURCE = Source of data

C = Central/district/county office person

A = Administrator/counselor/public relations person

T = Teacher

S = Student

P = Parent

H = Arts area chairperson

V = Visit or tour of facility

Appendix C

Sample Participant Letter and Questionnaire

SAMPLE LETTER

Barbara Smith
5693 Mayflower Dr.
Mission Viejo, CA 94732

April 15, 2004

Dear Principal/Teacher:

All levels of education in California and across the country are in transition. Many schools in California are in the process of change or are at least considering some elements of change. Your school has been selected as one of 40 schools in Orange County to respond to a questionnaire assessing group behavior or norms existing in elementary schools. I am a doctoral candidate at the University of La Verne conducting research regarding behavioral norms and characteristics of restructuring. The perceptions of how principals and teachers "do business" at their sites is of critical importance to this educational study.

The following description of group behavior or norms may be helpful to you for the purpose of this study. Norms are the shared group expectations about behavior. They can be explicitly stated as rules or guidelines for behavior or can be implicitly understood as the way things happen in an organization. Norms can be productive or nonproductive regarding the goals of the organization.

Please complete this questionnaire assessing group behavior or norms in your school. It will only take a few minutes of your time. This three-part questionnaire asks you to respond to group behavior or norm statements about your school as well as to respond to the degree of involvement in restructuring.

Please complete and seal each questionnaire in the attached white envelope and return all questionnaires in the enclosed self-addressed, stamped large brown collection envelope no later than May 6th. All responses will remain confidential, and your anonymity will be ensured. Your responses will contribute to this timely research about school norms, restructuring, and change. A summary of the research will be mailed to you upon completion.

I appreciate your participation in this research.

Sincerely,

Lynn Bogart, Principal

Irvine Unified School District

SAMPLE QUESTIONNAIRE

Group Behaviors and Restructuring Questionnaire

Part 1

Please answer the following questions relative to the behaviors accepted by the staff as "the way things happen around here."

Directions

To what degree does each of the norms below operate in your school?

Please respond according to the following scale:

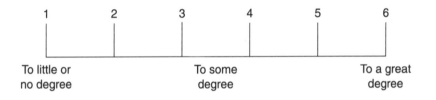

1	2	3	4	5	6

To little or
no degree

To some
degree

To a great
degree

Staff members may include certificated and classified personnel. Teachers refer to certificated personnel.

_____ 1. Staff members make suggestions in meetings.

_____ 2. Staff members informally discuss how they can make things better on this campus.

_____ 3. Systems for decision making are in place and known to staff members.

_____ 4. Staff members confront each other on issues.

_____ 5. Staff members try out new ideas.

_____ 6. Staff members do their own work without involving others.

_____ 7. Schoolwide decisions are made by using priority decision-making techniques.

_____ 8. Schoolwide decisions are made by consensus.

_____ 9. Teachers ask for help with specific instructional problems.

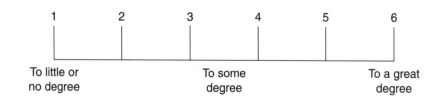

1	2	3	4	5	6

To little or
no degree

To some
degree

To a great
degree

_____ 10. Teachers work together to research materials and share ideas for curriculum.

_____ 11. Staff members are involved with important decisions.

_____ 12. Teachers discredit new ideas or programs.

_____ 13. Teachers design curriculum units on their own.

_____ 14. Staff members suggest agenda items for staff meetings.

_____ 15. Staff members describe to others an attempt to try something new.

_____ 16. Teachers review and discuss existing lesson plans with each other.

_____ 17. Solutions to problems that affect the school are determined primarily by the principal.

_____ 18. Teachers openly question classroom or schoolwide practices.

_____ 19. Teachers suggest that others "try this."

_____ 20. Teachers invite other teachers to observe them in their own classroom.

_____ 21. Parents participate in the decision-making process about schoolwide issues.

_____ 22. Staff members who disagree with a decision attempt to get it changed after the decision is made.

_____ 23. The staff accepts innovation.

_____ 24. Staff members work together to solve problems.

_____ 25. Staff members attempt to change unwanted decisions by going to sources outside the school.

_____ 26. Staff members support decisions made by the group, even when they feel another decision would be better.

_____ 27. It is important for innovations to be initially successful on this campus.

1	2	3	4	5	6

To little or
no degree

To some
degree

To a great
degree

_____ 28. Parent suggestions for changes at the school are accepted by the staff.

_____ 29. Conflict exists, but it is not discussed at school.

_____ 30. Staff members receive praise or recognition for trying new ideas.

_____ 31. Staff members share information to help others.

_____ 32. Staff members confront those who "don't do their share."

_____ 33. Staff members view mistakes or failures as opportunities to learn.

_____ 34. Staff members share information only when it benefits them.

_____ 35. Staff members complain about changes going on in the school.

_____ 36. Staff members are involved in solving curriculum and instructional problems.

_____ 37. Staff members try to keep things the same.

_____ 38. Conflict resolution is seen as a positive activity.

_____ 39. Staff members help others put new ideas into practice.

_____ 40. Staff members know the processes used for resolving conflicts.

_____ 41. Staff members resist putting new ideas into practice.

_____ 42. Teachers persuade others to try an idea or approach.

_____ 43. Teachers make collective agreements to participate in programs.

_____ 44. Parents openly question schoolwide practices.

Part 2

1. Many schools in California are involved in some form of school reform or restructuring, while several have chosen not to be

involved at this time. Using the scale directly below, *to what degree is your school involved* in reform or restructuring? Indicate your response here. _____

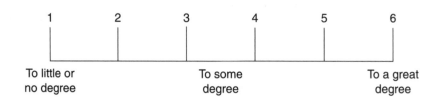

2. If participating in restructuring, how many years has your school been involved? _____ year(s)

3. What is your role in the school? Teacher _____ Principal _____

4. How many years have you been working at this school? _____

Part 3

Directions

Below is a list of characteristics which may or may not describe your school. Regardless of how you answered the previous restructuring questions, please respond to what degree each of these characteristics reflect the current condition of your school. Please consider each item independently of the others. Do not allow the way you mark one item to affect the way you mark another item.

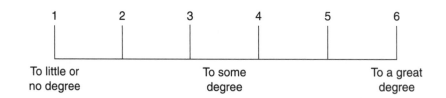

_____ 1. Existence of a clear, shared, results-oriented vision

_____ 2. Support for the value of learning at all levels of the organization

_____ 3. Support for the change process

_____ 4. Support for continuous improvement

_____ 5. Focus on high-level thinking and problem solving

_____ 6. Implementation of instructional strategies based on current learning theory

_____ 7. Emphasis on real-life performance assessments of student learning

_____ 8. Support for discarding or reforming existing structures or forms such as use of time, space, schedules, groupings, etc.

_____ 9. Existence of shared leadership in decision-making and problem-solving processes

Thank you very much for your time in responding to this questionnaire. Please put your completed questionnaire in the white envelope attached to the form. Seal the white envelope and place it in the large brown collection envelope. To protect the confidentiality of your responses, the white envelopes will be opened only by the researcher.

SOURCE: Bogart, L., *Identification of Behavioral Norms in Restructuring and Traditional Schools,* doctoral dissertation, University of La Verne, 1995. Reprinted with permission.

Appendix D: Sample Table—Presenting the Results

Number and Percentage of Teachers and Principals Reporting the Presence of Risk-Taking Norms According to Three Categories of School Restructuring

Norm Statement (Listed by questionnaire item number)		Traditional Teachers N = 70 Principals N = 10 Scale Ratings						Middle Group Teachers N = 131 Principals N = 17 Scale Ratings						Restructuring Teachers N = 96 Principals N = 12 Scale Ratings					
		6–5		4–3		2–1		6–5		4–3		2–1		6–5		4–3		2–1	
		N	%	N	%	N	%	N	%	N	%	N	%	N	%	N	%	N	%
1. Staff members make suggestions in meetings.	T	48	68.5	22	31.5	0	0	109	83.2	20	15.3	2	1.5	86	89.6	10	10.5	0	0
	P	8	80.0	2	20.0	0	0	15	88.2	2	11.8	0	0	12	100.0	0	0	0	0
5. Staff members try out new ideas.	T	39	55.7	30	42.9	1	1.4	91	69.5	38	29.0	2	1.6	87	90.6	8	8.4	1	1.0
	P	4	40.0	6	60	0	0	11	64.7	6	35.3	0	0	11	91.7	1	8.3	0	0
9. Teachers ask for help with specific instructional problems.	T	23	32.8	38	54.3	9	12.9	63	48.1	54	41.2	14	10.7	62	64.6	34	35.5	0	0
	P	2	20.0	7	70.0	1	10.0	8	47.1	8	47.0	1	5.9	5	41.7	6	50.0	1	8.3
12. Teachers do not discredit new ideas or programs.	T	36	51.5	29	41.4	5	7.1	77	58.8	44	33.6	10	7.17	70	72.9	19	19.8	7	7.3
	P	9	90.0	1	10.0	0	0	8	47.0	9	52.9	0	0	11	91.6	1	8.3	0	0
15. Staff members describe to others an attempt to try something new.	T	1.9	27.1	42	60.0	9	1.9	59	45.01	68	51.9	4	3.1	57	59.3	39	40.7	0	0
	P	4	40.0	5	50.0	1	10.0	6	35.3	8	47.1	3	17.6	7	58.4	5	41.6	0	0
19. Teachers suggest that others "try this."	T	21	30.0	38	54.3	11	15.7	50	38.2	69	52.7	12	9.2	44	45.9	42	54.1	0	0
	P	2	20.0	7	70.0	1	10.0	8	47.1	9	52.9	0	0	3	25.0	8	66.7	1	8.3
23. The staff accepts innovation.	T	21	30.0	38	54.3	11	15.8	65	49.6	60	45.8	6	4.6	72	75	24	25.1	0	0
	P	3	30.0	7	70.0	0	0	5	29.4	11	64.7	1	5.9	11	91.6	0	0	1	8.3

Categories of School Restructuring

SOURCE: Bogart, L., *Identification of Behavioral Norms in Restructuring and Traditional Schools*, doctoral dissertation, University of La Verne, 1995. Reprinted with permission.

Appendix E

Dissertation Content Checklist

Following are some questions to be considered when evaluating the quality and completeness of your own or others' dissertation document. Not all of the questions are appropriate for all studies, and some of the items within chapters may vary somewhat based on the preferences of the dissertation advisor.

Chapter 1

Statement of the Problem

1. Is the background of the problem clearly presented?

2. Is adequate background presented for all the variables or concepts under study?

3. Is adequate information presented for an understanding of the problem?

4. Is the problem clearly stated?

5. Is there a need to know?

6. Is it clear how this study will add to the body of knowledge (theory or practice)?

7. Is the theoretical base for the study clear and appropriate?

8. Is there an appropriate amount of literature cited?

9. Is there an indication of what's known and what's not known about the variables under investigation?

10. Is there a description and an analysis of what has already been done related to the problem?

11. Is the relationship of the problem to previous research made clear?

12. Is there a logical sequence of exposition that leads directly to the purpose statement?

13. Is the writing clear and readable?

14. Does the chapter move from the general to the specific?

Purpose Statement

15. Is the purpose of the study stated clearly and succinctly?

16. Is the purpose related to the problem statement?

Research Questions

17. Are the research questions well stated?
    - o Clear variables
    - o No *how* or *why* questions
    - o "Thing" words clarified (*success, factors, achievement,* etc.)

18. Is the kind of measurement obvious? (description, differences, or relationship)

Delimitations: The Boundaries of the Study

19. Are delimitations well defined? (timeframe, location, sample, criterion, etc.)

20. Are the author's assumptions made clear?

Significance of the Study: So What?

21. Is there an explanation of how the study will be useful to knowledge, practitioners, or policy makers?

Definition of Terms: Terms Used in the Study That Do Not Have Commonly Known Meanings

22. Are the terms used in the study adequately defined so that their usage is understood?

Chapter 2

Review of the Literature

23. Is the review of the literature comprehensive? (i.e., Does it cover the major points of the topic?)

24. Is there a balanced coverage of all variables or concepts in the study?

25. Have the majority of references been published within the past five years?

26. Does the bibliography contain at least 40 to 60 references?

27. Is the review well organized? Does it flow logically?

28. Are authors who make the same point combined in the citation?

29. Does the author critically analyze the literature rather than string together a series of citations?

30. Is there a summary at the end of each major section as well as at the end of the chapter?

31. Is there an organizing principle evident in the review? A story line? (e.g., "Four schools of thought . . ." "Six themes that emerge . . ." "Acorn to oak")

32. Do the direct quotations detract from the readability of the chapter?

33. Is there an overabundance of paraphrasing or direct quotations?

Chapter 3

Methodology

Kind of Research

34. Is the kind of research and research design described fully? (case study, descriptive, experimental, etc.)

35. Are the variables clearly described?

36. Is the design appropriate for testing the research questions of the study?

37. Is the methodology reported in sufficient detail that you could replicate the study without further information?

38. If case study was the methodology used, were criteria for selecting the cases clearly stated?

Sample and Population

39. Was the entire population studied? Was a sample selected?

40. Was the kind of sampling used described adequately? (simple random, stratified random, cluster sampling, purposive sampling, etc.)

41. Was the sample size large enough?

42. Are the size and major characteristics of the sample described adequately?

43. Are the procedures for selecting a sample clearly described?

44. Are criteria for selecting the sample stated?

Instrumentation

45. Is a rationale given for the selection of the instruments used?

46. Is each instrument described in terms of purpose and content?

47. Are the instruments appropriate for measuring the variables?

48. If an instrument was developed specifically for the study, are the procedures involved in its development and validation described?

49. If an instrument was developed specifically for the study, are the administration, scoring, and interpretation procedures fully described?

50. Is instrument validity discussed? *Validity* = the degree to which the instrument consistently measures what it purports to measure.

51. Are reliability procedures discussed? *Reliability* = the degree to which the instrument consistently measures something from one time to another. If measured again, would you find the same results?

52. If interviews were used to collect data, were procedures described for detecting interviewer bias?

53. Were interobserver or interrater reliability assessed? Was satisfactory interrater reliability found?

Data Collection and Procedures

54. Are procedures for collecting data described in sufficient detail to permit them to be replicated by another researcher?

55. Was a pilot study conducted?

56. If a pilot study was conducted, are its execution and results described?

57. Are the following data collection procedures described?
    o Statement of how and when data were collected?
    o Follow-up procedures?
    o Timeline?
    o Computer support?

58. If the study was qualitative, were internal validity strategies described? (triangulation, member checks, peer examination, etc.)

Data Analysis

59. Were the statistics appropriate for the study?

60. Are the appropriate statistics reported for each test?

61. For statistical tests, are enough statistics (mean, standard deviation, etc.) presented?

62. In a qualitative study, are the themes and patterns appropriately labeled?

Limitations: Weaknesses of the Study

63. Are the limitations of the study clearly delineated?

64. Are methodological weaknesses of the study discussed?

Chapter 4

Findings

65. Are the findings presented clearly?

66. Are the findings presented in relation to the research questions?

67. Are tables, figures, and so on, if used, well organized and easy to understand?

68. Does each table, if used, stand on its own, clear and self-explanatory?

69. Are the notable data in each table and figure described in the text?

70. Is this section free of interpretation? (Note: In historical, case study, or ethnographic studies, factual and interpretive material is sometimes interwoven to sustain interest.)

71. Within the themes and patterns of a qualitative study, is there a balance of direct quotations and description to enhance the meaning of the themes and patterns?

72. Is there a summary of the key findings?

Chapter 5

Summary, Conclusions, and Recommendations

Summary

73. Is there a brief summary of the problem, the methodology, and the findings?

Conclusions: What Does It Mean?

74. Are conclusions clearly stated?

75. Are conclusions derived from the findings?

76. Are conclusions mere restatements of the findings?

77. Are conclusions discussed within the framework of previous studies, theory, and the literature base?

78. Are generalizations made that are not warranted by the findings?

79. Are generalizations confined to the population from which the sample was drawn?

Recommendations: What Should Be Done?

80. Are recommendations for action stated? (e.g., practical suggestions for practitioners, theory, or policy makers)

81. Are suggestions for action made that are not justified by the data?

82. Are recommendations for future research made?

Bibliography

Abascal, J. R., Brucato, D., & Brucato, L. (2001). *Stress mastery, the art of coping gracefully.* Upper Saddle River, NJ: Prentice Hall.

American Psychological Association. (2010). *Publication manual of the American Psychological Association* (6th ed.). Washington, DC: Author.

Azuma, R. (2002). *Everything I wanted to know about C.S. graduate school at the beginning but didn't learn until later.* Retrieved August 15, 2002, from http://www.cs.unc.edu/~ azuma/hitch4.html

Babbie, E. (2001). *Survey research methods* (9th ed.). Belmont, CA: Wadsworth.

Balian, E. S. (1994). *The graduate research guidebook: A practical approach to doctoral/masters research.* Lanham, MD: University Press of America.

Best, S., & Krueger, B. (2004). *Internet data collection (quantitative applications in the Social Sciences).* Thousand Oaks, CA: Sage.

Bogart, L. (1995). *Identification of behavioral norms in restructuring and traditional schools.* Doctoral dissertation, University of La Verne.

Bogdan, R. C., & Biklen, S. K. (1992). *Qualitative research for education: An introduction to theory and methods.* Boston: Allyn & Bacon.

Bolker, J. (1998). *Writing your dissertation in fifteen minutes a day.* New York: Henry Holt.

Boote, D., & Beile, P. (2005). Scholars before researchers: On the centrality of the dissertation literature review in research preparation. *Educational Researcher, 34*(6), 3–15.

Booth, W. C., Colomb, G. G., & Williams, J. M. (1995). *The craft of research.* Chicago: University of Chicago Press.

Borg, W. R., & Gall, M. D. (1983). *Educational research* (4th ed.). New York: Longman.

Boullion, B. M. (1996). *Socialization experiences of beginning elementary principals in selected California school districts.* Doctoral dissertation, University of La Verne.

Bounford, T., & Alastair, C. (2000). *Digital diagrams: How to design and present statistical information effectively.* New York: Watson-Guptill.

Butt, M. (1993). *What do superintendents do to turn vision into action? A biography of pragmatic visionaries.* Doctoral dissertation, University of La Verne.

Chaffee, C. (1995). *Initiating reform in California public elementary schools.* Unpublished doctoral dissertation, University of La Verne.

Clark, R. (2002). *Components of selected public-private partnerships to build new schools in California.* Doctoral dissertation, University of La Verne.

Coffey, A., & Atkinson, P. (1996). *Making sense of qualitative data.* Thousand Oaks, CA: Sage.

Coleman, M., & Briggs, A. R. (Eds.). (2002). *Research methods in educational leadership and management.* London: Paul Chapman.

Cooper, D. (1992). *A case study of the perceived characteristics and life events that enabled four women to become university presidents.* Doctoral dissertation, University of La Verne.

Corbin, J., & Strauss, A. (2008). *Basics of qualitative research* (3rd ed.). Thousand Oaks, CA: Sage.

Costa, A. L., & Garmston, R. (1994). *Cognitive coaching.* Norwood, MA: Christopher-Gordon.

Council of Graduate Schools. (2002). *The role and nature of the doctoral dissertation: A policy statement.* Retrieved from http://cgsnet.org/Publications PolicyRes/role.htm

Couper, M. (2008). *Designing effective web surveys.* New York: Cambridge University Press.

Cox, J. (1996). *Your opinion, please! How to build the best questionnaires in the field of education.* Thousand Oaks, CA: Corwin.

Cox, J., & Cox, K. (2007). *Your opinion, please! How to build the best questionnaires in the field of education* (2nd ed.). Thousand Oaks, CA: Corwin.

Creswell, J. W. (2002). *Research design: Qualitative, quantitative, and mixed methods approaches* (2nd ed.). Thousand Oaks, CA: Sage.

Creswell, J. W. (2005). *Educational research: Planning, conducting, and evaluating quantitative and qualitative research* (2nd ed.). Upper Saddle River, NJ: Pearson/Merrill Prentice Hall.

Creswell, J. W. (2008). *Educational research: Planning, conducting, and evaluating quantitative and qualitative research* (3rd ed.). Upper Saddle River, NJ: Pearson/Merrill Prentice Hall.

Creswell, J. W. (2009). *Research design: Qualitative, quantitative, and mixed methods approaches.* (3rd ed.).Thousand Oaks, CA: Sage.

Creswell, J. W., & Plano Clark, V. L. (2007). *Designing and conducting mixed methods research.* Thousand Oaks, CA: Sage.

Danziger, E. (2001). *Get to the point.* New York: Three Rivers.

Daumal, R. (1952). *Mount Analogue.* New York: Overlook.

Daumal, R. (1986). *Mount Analogue.* New York: Penguin.

Denzin, N. K., & Lincoln, Y. S. (Eds.). (2000). *Handbook of qualitative research.* Thousand Oaks, CA: Sage.

Denzin, N. K., & Lincoln, Y. S. (Eds.). (2005). *The SAGE handbook of qualitative research* (3rd ed.). Thousand Oaks, CA: Sage.

Dillman, D. A. (1999). *Mail and Internet surveys: The tailored design method.* New York: John Wiley.

Fink, A. (2010). *Conducting research literature reviews.* Thousand Oaks, CA: Sage.

Fitzpatrick, J., Secrist, J., & Wright, D. J. (1998). *Secrets for a successful dissertation.* Thousand Oaks, CA: Sage.

Fowler, F. J. (2002). *Survey research methods* (3rd ed.). Thousand Oaks, CA: Sage.

Freedman, D., Pisani, R., & Purves, R. (1998). *Statistics.* London: W. W. Norton.

Galvan, J. (2006). *Writing literature reviews.* Glendale, CA: Pyrczak Publishing.

Garcia-Lipscomb, L. L. (1997). *The effect of faculty/administrator collective bargaining strategies on California community college climates.* Doctoral dissertation, University of La Verne.

Garmston, R., & Hyerle, D. (1988). *Professor's peer coaching program: Report on a 1987–88 pilot project to develop and test a staff development model for improving instruction at California State University, Sacramento, CA.*

Gay, L. R., & Airasian, P. (1996). *Educational research.* Columbus, OH: Merrill Prentice Hall.

Gay, L. R., & Airasian, P. (2003). *Educational research: Competencies for analysis and applications.* Columbus, OH: Merrill Prentice Hall.

Gay, L. R., Mills, G., & Peter, A. (2008). *Educational research: Competencies for analysis and applications* (9th ed.). Upper Saddle River, NJ: Merrill Prentice Hall.

Geery, L. (1997). *An exploratory study of the ways in which superintendents use their emotional intelligence to address conflict in their organizations.* Doctoral dissertation, University of La Verne.

Glatthorn, A. A. (1998). *Writing the winning dissertation.* Thousand Oaks, CA: Corwin.

Goehring, H. J. (1981). *Statistical methods in education.* Arlington, VA: Information Resources Press.

Gonzales, L. (2002). *Inspiring the pinch hitters—Job satisfaction and dissatisfaction of substitute teachers.* Doctoral dissertation, University of La Verne.

Green, J. C., & Caracelli, V. J. (Eds). (1997). *Advances in mixed-method evaluation: The challenges and benefits of integrating diverse paradigm.* New Directions for Evaluation, 74. San Francisco: Jossey-Bass.

Griessman, B. E. (1994). *Time tactics of very successful people.* New York: McGraw-Hill.

Hacker, D. (2007). *A writer's reference* (6th ed.). Boston: Bedford/St. Martin's.

Harmon, C. (Ed.). (2000). *Using the Internet, online services, and CD-ROMs for writing research and term papers.* New York: Neal-Schuman.

Hart, C. (1998). *Doing a literature review: Releasing the social science research imagination.* Thousand Oaks, CA: Sage.

Hart, C. (2004). *Doing a literature search: A comprehensive guide for the social sciences.* Thousand Oaks, CA: Sage.

Hernandez, A. (1996). *A comparative study of the leadership orientation frames of public and non-public special education.* Doctoral dissertation, University of La Verne.

Isaac, S., & Michael, W. B. (1995). *Handbook in research and evaluation.* San Diego, CA: EdITS/Educational and Industrial Testing Services.

Johnston, B. (2000). *The effects of looping on parent involvement and student attitudes in elementary classrooms.* Doctoral dissertation, University of La Verne.

Kinley, K. E. (1996). *Changes which occurred at three California middle schools where school-linked services were delivered.* Dissertation, University of La Verne.

Klausmeier, H. J. (2001). *Research writing in education and psychology—From planning to publication.* Springfield, IL: Charles C Thomas.

Lakein, A. (1996). *How to get control of your time and your life.* New York: Signet.

Lewis-Beck, M. S. (Ed.). (1994). *Basic statistics.* International Handbooks of Quantitative Applications in the Social Sciences (Vol. 1). London: Sage.

Lightfoot, S. L. (1985). *The good high school: Portraits of character and culture.* New York: Basic Books.

Madsen, D. (1992). *Successful dissertations and theses.* San Francisco: Jossey-Bass.

Marsh, C. (2009). *Exploring data: An introduction to data analysis for social scientists* (2nd ed.). New York: Blackwell.

Marshall, C., & Rossman, G. B. (1999). *Designing qualitative research* (3rd ed.). Thousand Oaks, CA: Sage.

Martin, R. (1980). *Writing and defending a thesis or dissertation in psychology and education.* Springfield, IL: Charles C Thomas.

Maslow, A. H. (1968). *Toward a psychology of being.* New York: Van Nostrand Reinhold.

Mauch, J., & Birch, J. W. (1993). *Guide to the successful thesis and dissertation.* New York: Marcel Dekker.

Melendrez, D. (1991). *Realizing the dream: A case study of California arts high schools.* Doctoral dissertation, University of La Verne.

Merriam, S. B. (2001). *Qualitative research and case study applications in education.* San Francisco: Jossey-Bass.

Mertens, D. M. (1998). *Research methods in education and psychology: Integrating diversity with quantitative and qualitative approaches.* Thousand Oaks, CA: Sage.

Miles, M. B., & Huberman, A. M. (1988). *Qualitative data analysis: An expanded sourcebook.* Thousand Oaks, CA: Sage.

Miles, M. B., & Huberman, A. M. (1994). *Qualitative data analysis: An expanded sourcebook.* Thousand Oaks, CA: Sage.

Miller, J. I., & Taylor, B. J. (1987). *The thesis writer's handbook.* West Linn, OR: Alcove.

Miranda, F. (1993). *The effects of year round education on limited English proficient (LEP) students in two California high schools.* Doctoral dissertation, University of La Verne.

Munter, M. (1997). *Guide to managerial communication.* Upper Saddle River, NJ: Prentice Hall.

Murray, D. M. (1995). *The craft of revision.* Orlando, FL: Harcourt Brace.

Nesbary, D. (1999). *Survey research and the World Wide Web.* Boston: Allyn & Bacon.

Neuman, W. L. (2005). *Social research methods: Qualitative and quantitative approaches* (6th ed.). Boston: Allyn & Bacon.

Nevills, P. (1995). *A developmental study of a professional development training program designed to prepare a cadre of educators for school site change facilitation.* Doctoral dissertation, University of La Verne.

Newman, I., & Benz, C. R. (1998). *Qualitative-quantitative research methodology: Exploring the interactive continuum.* Carbondale: Southern Illinois University Press.

O'Conner, P. (1996). *Woe is I: The grammarphobe's guide to better English in plain English* (3rd ed.). New York: Riverhead.

Ó Dochartaigh, N. (2007). *Internet research skills.* London, England: Sage.

Ogden, E. (1993). *Completing your doctoral dissertation or master's thesis in two semesters or less.* Lancaster, PA: Technomic.

Oliver, P. (2008). *The student's guide to research ethics.* New York: Open University Press.

Pascarelli, E. (2004). *Dr. Pascarelli's complete guide to repetitive strain injury: What you need to know about RSI and Carpal Tunnel Syndrome.* New York: John Wiley.

Patton, M. Q. (2002). *Qualitative research & evaluation methods* (3rd ed.). Thousand Oaks, CA: Sage.

Piantanida, M., & Garman, N. B. (1999). *The qualitative dissertation: A guide for students and faculty.* Thousand Oaks, CA: Corwin.

Reichardt, C. S., & Rallis, S. E. (Eds.). (1994). *The qualitative-quantitative debate: New perspectives.* New Directions for Program Evaluation, 61. San Francisco: Jossey-Bass.

Remenyi, D., Williams, B., Money, A., & Swartz, E. (1998). *Doing research in business and management: An introduction to process and method.* Newbury Park, CA: Sage.

Richardson, M. D., & Prickett, R. L. (1991). *Publication sources in educational leadership.* Lancaster, PA: Technomic.

Ridley, D. (2008). *The literature review: A step-by-step guide for students.* Thousand Oaks, CA: Sage.

Roig, M. (2006). *Avoiding plagiarism, self-plagiarism, and other questionable writing practices: A guide to ethical writing.* Retrieved January 2009 from http://facpub.stjohns.edu/~roigm/plagiarism/Index.html

Rossman, G. B., & Rallis, S. F. (1998). *Learning in the field: An introduction to qualitative research.* Thousand Oaks, CA: Sage.

Rossman, G. B., & Rallis, S. F. (2003). *Learning in the field: An introduction to qualitative research* (2nd ed.). Thousand Oaks, CA: Sage.

Rudestam, K. E., & Newton, R. R. (1992). *Surviving your dissertation: A comprehensive guide to content and process.* Newbury Park, CA: Sage.

Rudestam K. E., & Newton, R. R. (2007). *Surviving your dissertation: A comprehensive guide to content and process* (3rd ed.). Thousand Oaks, CA: Sage.

Schuller, R. H. (1980*). The peak to peek principle.* New York: Bantam.

Schultz, B. (2008). *Freshmen adjustment to college at the University of Alaska: A descriptive ex post facto study.* Doctoral dissertation, University of La Verne.

Shulman, M. (2005). *In focus: Strategies for academic writers.* Ann Arbor: University of Michigan Press.

Sieber, J. (1992). *Planning ethically responsible research: A guide for students and internal review boards.* Newbury Park, CA: Sage.

Silverman, D. (1993). *Interpreting qualitative data.* London: Sage.

Spindle, B. (2006). *A study of Alaska native student persistence and academic success at the University of Alaska Anchorage.* Doctoral dissertation, University of La Verne.

Staindack, S., & Staindack, W. (1988). *Understanding & conducting qualitative research.* Dubuque, IA: Kendall/Hunt.

Stake, R. E. (1994). Case studies. In N. K. Denzin & Y. S. Lincoln (Eds.), *Handbook of qualitative research.* Thousand Oaks, CA: Sage.

Sternberg, D. (1981). *How to complete and survive a doctoral dissertation.* New York: St.Martin's.

Stone, W. C. (1962). *The success system that never fails.* New York: Pocket Books.

Strauss, A., & Corbin, J. (1990). *Basics of qualitative research.* Newbury Park, CA: Sage.

Strausser, J. (2001). *Painless writing.* New York: Barron's.

Strong, W. S. (1998). *The copyright book: A practical guide.* Cambridge, MA: MIT Press.

Strunk, W., & White, E. B. (1979). *The elements of style* (3rd ed.). New York: Macmillan.

Strunk, W., & White, E. B. (2000). *The elements of style* (4th ed.). Boston: Allyn & Bacon.

Sue, V. (2007). *Conducting online surveys.* Thousand Oaks, CA: Sage.

Tashakkori, A., & Teddlie, C. (1998). *Mixed methodology: Combining qualitative and quantitative approaches.* Thousand Oaks, CA: Sage.

Tashakkori, A., & Teddlie, C. (Eds.). (2003). *Handbook of mixed methods in the social and behavioral sciences.* Thousand Oaks, CA: Sage.

Tesch, R. (1990). *Qualitative research: Analysis types and software tools.* New York: Falmer.

Tuckman, B. W. (1999). *Conducting educational research* (5th ed.). Fort Worth, TX: Harcourt Brace.

Tufte, E. R. (2001). *The visual display of quantitative information.* Cheshire, CT: Graphics Press.

Turabian, K. L. (1996). *A manual for writers of term papers, theses, and dissertations* (6th ed.). Chicago: University of Chicago Press.

United States Department of Health and Human Services, Code of Federal Regulations 45 CFR 46.116(a), pages 14–15.

University of Chicago Press. (1993). *The Chicago manual of style: The essential guide for writers, editors, and publishers* (14th ed.). Chicago: Author.

Venolia, J. (2001). *Write right! A desktop digest of punctuation, grammar, and style.* Berkeley, CA: Ten Speed Press.

Waitley, D. (1987). *Being the best.* Nashville, TN: Oliver Nelson.

Walkington, B. A. (1991). *Strategies principals use to implement shared decision making.* Doctoral dissertation, University of La Verne.

Weitzman, E., & Miles, W. B. (1995). *Computer programs for qualitative data analysis: A software sourcebook.* Thousand Oaks, CA: Sage.

Western Association of Schools and Colleges. (2008). *Handbook of accreditation of the Western Association of Schools and Colleges.* Alameda, CA: Author.

Wilkinson, A. M. (1991). *The scientist's handbook for writing papers and dissertations.* Englewood Cliffs, NJ: Prentice Hall.

Wolcott, H. F. (2001). *Writing up qualitative research* (2nd ed.). Thousand Oaks, CA: Sage.

Wright, K. B. (2005). Researching Inter-based populations: Advantages and disadvantages of online survey research, online questionnaire authoring software packages, and web survey services. *Journal of Computer-Mediated Communication, 10*(3), Article 11. Available from http://jcmc.indiana.edu/vol10/issue3/wright.html

Zinsser, W. (1994). *On writing well: An informal guide to writing nonfiction* (5th ed.). NewYork: HarperPerennial.

Helpful Websites

Dissertation Doctor: www.dissertationdoctor.com

Association for Support of Graduate Students (ASGS): www.asgs.org
    The following services are offered:

- *Thesis News.* A news and reference bulletin for graduate students writing their theses or dissertations.
- *Professional Consultant Directory.* A listing of format editors, statistical consultants, typists, and so on.

The Elements of Style by William Strunk: http://bartelby.com/141

The Writing Center, University of North Carolina: www.unc.edu/depts/wcweb/handouts/dissertation.html

Index

CORWIN

A SAGE Company

The Corwin logo—a raven striding across an open book—represents the union of courage and learning. Corwin is committed to improving education for all learners by publishing books and other professional development resources for those serving the field of PreK–12 education. By providing practical, hands-on materials, Corwin continues to carry out the promise of its motto: **"Helping Educators Do Their Work Better."**